Design Education in Craft and Technology

The Proceedings of the 1976 Northampton Conference

edited by
F. R. Willmore

Editorial Board:
K. Jennings
E. Swithinbank

B. T. BATSFORD LTD. London

The proceedings of the 1976 Annual Conference of the Institute of Craft Education were held at Nene College, Northampton, in April 1976. The officers of the Conference were:

R. Heaton President 1975-6
K. Jennings Chairman, 1976 Conference Committee
F.R. Willmore Editor, 1976 Conference Publications

© Institute of Craft Education/B T Batsford Ltd 1976
First published in 1976

Printed by Billing & Son Ltd, Worcester
for the Publishers B T Batsford Ltd
4 Fitzhardinge Street, London W1H OAH
in collaboration with the Institute of Craft Education
3 Leabourne Road, London N16 6SX

ISBN 0 7134 3178 (cased)
     0 7134 3177 6 (limp)

Contents

Acknowledgment

The editors wish to thank the authors for their co-operation in maintaining the tight schedule demanded by the exercise. Thanks also go to the editorial staff of B T Batsford Ltd for their generous and helpful encouragement and their efficient and untiring work at all stages of the production. To prepare and publish a work of this nature in the short time available is no mean publishing feat. We offer to all engaged on the production of the work our congratulations and our gratitude.

Introduction

The Institute of Craft Education is the professional association of teachers of craft, design and technology subjects in schools in the United Kingdom. It has members working in, and contributing to, the creative, technical and practical areas of schools and colleges. Through its branch meetings, publications and conferences, the Institute maintains a dialogue and provides a platform for discussion and debate on matters relating to its specific interests and concern. Over the many years of its history it has contributed to curricular development and reform in the field of its specialism. Members of the Institute have seen the change from 'manual instruction' through 'handicraft' to 'craft education' and, in choosing to debate design education at their 1976 conference they provide an opportunity to focus attention on such fundamental and practical problems connected with, and occasioned by, the current switch in emphasis from craft to design.

The Institute recognizes contemporary trends in the practical side of school education. 'Design education' is a term that is being increasingly used to describe a wide range and variety of educative experiences in schools in the United Kingdom. The subject area frequently consists of an expansion of the work of the traditional crafts with incursions into art on the one hand, into science on the other, and with overtones of social and environmental studies. The trend of emphasis towards design as an integrating theme is influenced by a number of factors. The emergence of technology as a school subject, new and trial examinations, new teaching methods and strategies, and contemporary school building designs offering a wider variety of facilities and equipment for manipulating materials, have all influenced the change. Such considerations, together with the needs of pupils in a changing society, have extended the boundaries and underlying philosophy of the practical aspects of school education. At a time when the whole subject area is in a state of flux, it is appropriate that an attempt be made to synthesize experienced opinion and to objectively consider the aims and implications of design education.

Papers were invited from all authoritative sources; from the major research project teams, from colleges of education concerned with the training of teachers of the subject, and from individual contributors as well as from Institute members. The resulting statements published here represent a wide range of experience, ideas and comments of leading educationists working both inside and outside the classrooms, workshops and studios of our schools. Each paper represents the personal view of the contributor and, as a conference paper, is presented to inform, stimulate ideas and promote discussion. No attempt is made to classify them and they appear on these pages in the alphabetical order of the name of the contributor.

The further proceedings of the conference and reports of the ensuing deliberations and discussions will be reported in future editions of the Institute's journal — *Practical Education.* In offering this publication to a wider public, the Institute of Craft Education hopes that it will act not only as a record of informed and authoritative thinking at this time but also that it will initiate a wider debate and thereby contribute to a clearer definition of the direction and a deliniation of subject boundaries, thus leading to the formulation of a positive approach to the aims and methods of this essential area of the curriculum.

F.R.W.

1

The ambiguities of self-expression

R. T. ALLEN

R. T. Allen lectures in education and religious studies at Loughborough College of Education. He has published articles on aesthetics and the philosophy of education. He is currently organizing a colloquium on 'The Aesthetics of Craft' for the British Society of Aesthetics to be held at Loughborough during October/November 1976.

Abstract   The notion of self-expression is incoherent and anti-educational because (i) each of us has several selves or aspects, which may conflict, and the phrase does not tell us *which* to express; (ii) however, there is a tacit assumption that only the *artistic* self is to be expressed, and this is quite arbitrary; (iii) the ideology of self-expression is a democratization of the notion of the Original Genius, but does not allow that clumsiness and ineptness may count as self-expression; (iv) urging a child to express himself is either redundant or entails that what the child does is thereby *not* self-expression; (v) children have no fixed and determinate selves to express but are in the making; (vi) all children have imitative tendencies, and following is both self-expression (the expression of the *imitative* self) and yet not self-expression (but copying another); (vii) the whole ideology by-passes the question of value: the expression of a *bad* self is as much self-expression as that of a good self; (viii) and it is arbitrary to assume that *all* children will express themselves by means of education, literacy, articulateness and knowledge, but since we are born ignorant, illiterate and inarticulate *these* characteristics have a better claim to be self-expression than their opposites which have to be acquired by means of imitation and tuition.

Few of the catch-phrases that have figured in educational discussion have more dangerously anti-educational implications than that of 'self-expression', when it is used to denote an aim in teaching or a desired state of affairs in the classroom. Though today the phrase itself is not so evident as it used to be, and though a political vocabulary of 'rights', 'freedom' and 'authority' has, in progressivist ideology, largely superseded the notions of self-expression, growth, development and 'leading-out' (from the non-existent word *educere*), yet the idea is still with us, and an exposure of its ambiguities, indeed incoherence, is by no means superfluous. I shall endeavour to explicate the faulty logic of the term and to reveal the distortions which it can bring to thought about education and teaching, and hence into the practice of education.

Above the level of everyday work in schools, and of detailed and empirical research into the concrete tasks and performances of teachers and pupils, there is that of the ideas that control or influence our whole conception of education and the teacher's role, a level none the less real because less obvious and tangible. As the title of one of the most penetrating and incisive critiques of modern beliefs and assumptions stated, *Ideas Have Consequences*[1], for life and practice as well as for theory. Often a teacher's practice differs from his beliefs and his conception of what he is or should be doing, fortunately for his pupils. Indeed, I shall show that there *must* be such a difference in the case of self-expression. Nevertheless, a false or partial set of ideas can continue to distort, stunt or misdirect what he actually does in his teaching. A criticism of such beliefs and conceptions can restore native judgment and common sense, and can give us a renewed confidence in what we know to be sensible, possible and desirable.

The rhetoric of self-expression stems from the Romantic strain of progressivism, the tradition of Rousseau and Froebel, as distinct from the social, conformist and collectivist variety which originated with Dewey. The child, in the former view, is seen as radically pure and innocent; the prized qualities of self are spontaneity, freshness, individuality and creativity, and the aim is to allow, or to help, children to be themselves, in the belief that what is significant and of value comes forth from within and is not put into the child by the teacher. Like a plant, the child grows and develops, from within itself, upon its own and unique pattern, which must be tended and not stunted or twisted. Self-expression is both the end and the means, what the child should come to do and how he should arrive at the desired and final state. He should be *himself*, not an imitation of another. In contrast, the age-old aim and method of education has been to present the pupil with approved patterns of excellence, in crafts, thought, research, scholarship, art, manners, emotion and behaviour, to which he is directed and which he is expected to imitate and possess for himself. Recent attacks upon the belief in and use of paradigms as such take a political form: they are seen as social repression, class dominance, and élitism. Yet belief in the immediate and untutored expression of the self continues, and so do its pernicious effects.

I begin by quoting at length a superb passage from D.H. Lawrence, himself in most of his moods the most thorough-going exponent of the individualist and Romantic tradition in progressivism, yet also a critic of it, as here:

> Each child was to ex*press himself*: why, nobody thought necessary to explain. But infants were to express themselves, and nothing but themselves. Here was a pretty task for a teacher: he was to make his pupil *express himself*. Which *self* was left vague. A child was to be given a lump of soft clay and told to express himself, presumably in the pious hope that he might model a Tanagra figure or a Donatello plaque, all on his little lonely-o. Now it is obvious that every boy's first act of self-expression would be to throw the lump of soft clay at something: preferably at the teacher. This impulse was to be suppressed. On what grounds metaphysically? since the soft clay was given for self-expression. To this question there is just no answer. Self-expression in infants means, presumably, incipient Tanagra figurines and Dona-tello plaques, incipient *Iliad*s and *Macbeth*s and 'Odes to the Nightingale': a world of infant prodigies, in short.[2]

I shall now draw out the points made by Lawrence, though not in his order, and add some of my own.

1 'Which *self* was left vague'. We do not have each just one, uniform self, but several selves of different and sometimes conflicting aspects of the one self. Hence, 'self-expression' lacks an obvious reference. The command, 'express yourself', gives one no determinate task, for it leaves undefined *which* aspect of oneself or which self is to be expressed.

2 But there is an implicit restriction of choice of self, aspect of self or direction of expression: the instinct to throw the clay is to be inhibited, and only the *artistic* self is to be expressed[3]. But, on the metaphysics of self-expression, there is no justification for this restriction whatsoever: throwing clay is just as likely to express the pupil's self as using it for modelling, and more so if he, either now or in general, has no interest in modelling and has a real delight in throwing. Only upon some other and additional grounds can *any* restriction be justified. Moreover, just why should we automatically assume, as we do, that art and craft activities are the means and place for self-expression? Why cannot mathematics count as self-expression? Equally, it is taken for granted, in the view that equates teaching with therapy, that children will work off the frustrations induced by academic subjects in their art lessons, yet there is no idea that frustrations may be induced by the art lesson and assuaged in the laboratory or history room. An explanation of this automatic assumption is that this movement of educational thought has its logical and historical roots in Romanticism and began as a theory of artistic creation: that of the untaught and unspoiled Original Genius and art as 'the spontan-eous overflow of powerful emotions'. That self-expression is allowed to ruin only art and craft teaching may be something to be thankful for, but logic would require its extension right across the curriculum.

3 The ideology of self-expression is a democratization of the notion of the Original Genius: *all* children are artists and artists by instinct. Without the imitation of para-digms, without training and tuition, they are expected to produce 'Tanagra figures'

and 'Donatello plaques'. Lawrence may be attacking, in this case, a particular adjunct of the ideology, rather than the central belief, the extravagant hopes of some rather than the expectations of all. Nevertheless, *one* thing which none of the adherents of the ideology allow is that clumsiness and ineptness in art and craft should count as self-expression: either they do think that all children are born artists or they call art any daubings and scribblings produced by a child. Either they expect what cannot appear, or they abandon all aesthetic standards (or technical standards in crafts) in their ecstasy over the splashes and lumps produced by the child artist. (It is in any case dubious that there is often such a thing as children's *art*, that is, work produced *with an eye to* aesthetic effects, and not merely work produced for personal reasons – *'my* house', *'my* Mummy' – which *accidentally* has some aesthetic merit, recognizable by an adult and unseen by the child himself.) But again, there is no reason why clumsiness should not be reckoned as authentic self-expression.

4   More radically, why must the teacher *make* the pupil express himself? Either the child expresses himself without prompting, or he needs encouragement. In the first case, the teacher is superfluous; in the second, what results is surely *not* self-expression, for the child is doing whatever he is doing because his teacher has told or encouraged him to do it and not because it comes spontaneously to him. Hence, it is second-hand, another's idea and the execution of something which is not his own. Two paradoxes are present: the child, in being told to express himself, is given an abstract idea of himself and is made aware of himself and is encouraged to express himself *deliberately*; and also, any particular advice or materials given to the child to enable him to express himself must necessarily defeat the teacher's intention, for again the things suggested and provided come from another and at second-hand and not from the child, and what results is *not*, in this respect at least, the child's *own* work. Again, if self-expression really is the end, and the *only* end, teachers and teaching are redundant. In the former paradox, there is a contradiction between the aim of unreflective expression of what the child *is* and the cultivated expression of the child's *idea* of himself. For example, he may have no aesthetic interests and may like merely splashing around with paint, which then would count, or ought logically to count, as self-expression; but, told to express himself and made *aware* of himself, he may come to think of himself as an artist and deceive himself into thinking that he has got aesthetic interests, and so not splash around as he would if really left to himself, but affect an attention to artistic standards. What can self-expression be but the doing of what comes unthinkingly, and without prompting, and hence how can there be such a thing if children are not left *entirely* alone?

5   But, of course, children do not have determinate selves which merely await expression. Children are, necessarily, in the making and not made, as we all are to some extent. As any parent knows, children faced with a wet day to be spent indoors soon do not know what to do and ask for suggestions. Likewise, faced with blank paper they often have nothing to draw, and lack ideas. This must be the case at times, for, contrary to the metaphysics underlying self-expressionism, children have to *learn*, to acquire ideas and desires or more determinate desires rather than vague yearnings. The ideology of self-expression presupposes a Cartesian theory of innate ideas which need only to unfold. Daily observation of real children refutes that assumption. Self-expression is only possible when there is being and not becoming, a formed self and not one being formed.

6   A final incoherence in the very idea of self-expression is the problem of the imitative child who does *not* want to be himself but wishes to be like someone else, or to live as someone else wants him to live. All children, surely, have some model, real or imagined, which they wish to imitate, at least at certain points in their lives. Now if a child wishes to be like father, his best friend or even teacher, and if he acts accordingly, is this self-expression? On the one hand, it is *his* model of what he wants to be; on the other hand, he wants to be what he is not and to live according to a pattern set by

another. Moreover, since children are not born as Cartesian egos, it is inevitable that they should imitate others, especially adults. We can express the self-contradiction inherent in the idea by the case of the imitative child (and all children are imitative to some extent): if he copies another, then he does not express himself; but he *does* express himself, for his self *consists* of a tendency to imitate others. Imitation is not *self*-expression, but it *is* self-expression for it is the expression of an *imitative self*.

7   From these metaphysical heights, we now descend to more urgent matters of practice. We have noted that self-expression does not indicate *which* self is to be expressed. Now it is to be noted that the ideology by-passes the whole question of value and moral choice. Clearly, clay-throwing is not allowed to count as self-expression, not because it is not, but because the teacher will not like it. Likewise, art or craft activities are chosen rather than other things because the teacher likes them or thinks them worthwhile. If the reason is merely the personal preference of the teacher, then we have neither self-expression nor education. If the choice is made on the basis of the value of the activity, then that standard, whatever it may in fact be, is *external* to self-expression, otherwise the children would be allowed to do *whatever* they wished. Lawrence himself really did believe, much of the time, in the radical innocence of the child, indeed of the adult also: 'Nothing that comes from the deep passionate soul is bad or can be bad'[4]. In these moods, the value of what people did was irrelevant as far as he was concerned: anything and everything was permissible. Again, this is democratization of the idea of the Original Genius, transmuted into the 'beautiful soul', such as Rousseau's Julie who 'never had any other guide but her heart and could have no surer guide, . . . gives herself up to it without scruple, and to do right, has only to do all that it asks of her'[5]. What was originally the prerogative of the elect few, is now the right of all. If we repress bullying, then we do not believe in self-expression and its presupposition of the beautiful soul; if we believe in the latter, then we have no reason for inhibiting the self-expression of liars, thieves, cheats, thugs and vandals. Expression of a bad self is just as much expression as that of the good self.

8   Finally, there is a contradiction between the theory and practice of the believer in self-expression which he cannot escape while he continues as a teacher. Why does the self-expressionist assume that self-expression must take place in the context of education? Of course, the law constrains him, but logic does not. Lawrence did see this point and grasped the fundamentally anti-educational tendency of his beliefs: 'Is not radical *unlearnedness* just as true a form of self-expression, and just as desirable a state, for many natures (even the bulk), as learnedness?'[6] To be like Tennyson's animal that takes

> His license in the field of time,
> Unfetter'd by a sense of crime,
> To whom a conscience never wakes,

or to be a human cabbage may well be as authentic as any other modes of self-expression. Furthermore, there is usually a belief that all children are different on the part of adherents of self-expressionism and child-centred education in general: it is tacitly assumed that no one child's needs and interests will be like those of any other. If so, why should it be assumed that all require the context of education and schooling in order to express themselves? Again Lawrence drew the implications of his convictions: 'We talk about individuality, and try to drag up every weed into a rosebush. If a nettle likes to be a nettle, if it likes to have no flowers to speak of, why, that's the nettle's affair', and to force him to be otherwise (to make the child knowledgable, literate, skilful and articulate), is mere 'bullying idealism'[6]. Inarticulateness, illiteracy and ignorance cannot be ruled out *ab initio* and *ipso facto* as not being modes of self-expression. Moreover, since we are born ignorant, illiterate and inarticulate, they have a greater claim to being authentic modes than their opposites, which we cannot but acquire at second-hand, by tuition and by imitation.

Individualist progressivism, the child-centred ideology, feeds upon a largely mythical picture of traditional education as rigid drilling, wholly teacher-controlled, and sternly repressive, which it projects in order to justify its own reaction away from it to the opposite extreme of nerveless cringing before the child, formlessness and aimlessness. To criticize it in any way is to have the stereotype, composed of Gradgrind and Squeers, thrust upon one. Hence, I probably protest in vain that I do believe in the cultivation of imagination, emotion and sensibility, and that, since I believe in their *cultivation* (by active guidance and tuition on the part of the teacher), I have a better claim to believe in them than the adherents of an incoherent, antinomian and anti-educational self-expression.

Notes and References

1 Weaver R. *Ideas Have Consequences*, University of Chicago Press (1948)
2 Lawrence D.H. *Phoenix*, Macdonald Ed., p.594, Heinemann (1936)
3 See also the report on a summer school of the formidable college lecturer, Miss Crabbe, in 'Miss Read's' delightful *Storm in the Village*, Michael Joseph (1958): 'It deals with *every possible means* of self-expression, and we have tackled pottery-making, miming, finger-painting and stick-painting' (my emphasis).
4 Lawrence D.H. *Phoenix II*, Roberts and Moor Ed., p.276, Heinemann (1968)
5 Rousseau J.J. *Nouvelle Héloise*, Pt V, Lettre II
6 Lawrence D.H. *Phoenix*, Macdonald Ed, pp.595-6, Heinemann (1936)

2
Design in general education

B. AYLWARD

Bernard Aylward has been a member of the Institute of Craft Education for forty years. He has had experience of craft teaching, was Crafts Adviser in the West Riding and Leicestershire for over twenty-five years and served on the Consultative Committee of the Keele Project. Now retired, he is Chairman of the National Association for Design Education and a member of the Steering Committee of the Research Project, 'Design in General Education' at the Royal College of Art. He has contributed chapters to Attitudes in Design Education *and* Insights into Environmental Education *and has edited* Design Education in Schools. *He has frequently written articles for educational journals and is a regular speaker at educational conferences. He is still working as a craftsman and sculptor.*

Abstract   This paper explores and proposes answers to the following questions:
(i) What is design education? It is necessary first to establish what design education is. There is much confusion. Briefly it is the use educationally of the act of designing in order to understand society better.
(ii) What has caused this development? Design education is a natural development as a response to changes in society. Changes in social structure and in industry are demanding a higher level of understanding and responsibility and the need for *unthinking* manual skill is diminishing.
(iii) How does design education respond to changes? By putting emphasis on designing – without ignoring the educational value of craft skills – design education helps to develop the understanding and responsibility demanded. In order to understand a largely designed environment it is necessary to understand the act of designing.
(iv) What is the effect of design education on craft education? Design education can be seen as a logical extension of the traditional concern of the craft teacher to assist the social and moral development of his pupils through the act of creating. It is not in conflict with the essential aims of craft teaching but an opportunity to extend them.

I want to consider particularly the effect on crafts teaching of design education, but before doing so it is necessary to clarify what that phrase means since considerable confusion about it exists. To many it is simply another, trendy, name for art or handicraft. It is true that a strong tendency towards greater freedom of choice in work done and the need for more decision-making gives some justification for this. Yet this is a changed approach within an existing area of activity rather than the development of a new form of education.

The title is also used to denote a mixing of art, handicraft and home economics into one 'design department'. This certainly has a potential for change and development. The contact between teachers — as also found in departments of humanities and environmental education — can lead to a closer examination of work being done: a reappraisal of why we teach rather than how we teach, that is very beneficial. In many schools the contact between teachers fostered by the formation of design departments has led to more lively work. A willingness — essential to success — to answer, honestly, colleagues' queries as to why we do as we do, can help us to re-examine our aims. Of course sometimes, from lack of preparation, sound leadership, or willingness to co-operate, the formation of a design department can lead to chaos. But at its best, it will not automatically lead to sound design education unless there is an agreed plan to ensure that it does.

The first essential to successful planning is to ensure that pupils are given the opportunity to design. Here again we are up against a confusion in the use of terms. Quite legitimately the word 'design' can mean many different things, including a pattern to be applied to an artifact but this meaning is quite inadequate to support a form of education. The term 'basic design', coined for a 'basic' or 'foundation' course for designers in colleges of art and design is another trap for the unwary. Basic design is concerned with certain visual principles, such as colour, texture, form and spatial relationships. The understanding of these principles is, of course, essential to a designer, but in no sense do they provide him with the 'basis' for his work; they are only a foundation stone — one of many — on which he can build his expertise. To use such a course as the basis for the practical aspect of secondary education would be as absurd as diluting the first year of a degree course to cover the study of an academic subject over the same period.

Just as in craft education it is essential for pupils to act as craftsmen, so in design education it is essential for them to act as designers. Our understanding of the role of the designer has developed considerably over the last few years. At one time we thought of it as a simple decision-making activity that selected a different colour or form for something that was already being manufactured, but now we think of designing as something far more fundamental.

It is interesting, in this connection, to consider what professional designers consider their role to be. The last four annual conferences of the Society of Industrial Artists and Designers, which as a member I have attended, have been concerned to discuss this. They are obviously worried that they are often the agents for 'planned obsolescence': that they serve, merely, to titillate in order to maximize profits. They see their rightful role as that of humanizing technology; of making sure that whatever is manufactured is most acceptable and satisfying to mankind. The more one thinks of this the more important and central to society becomes the contribution of the designer.

Whatever the demands of his client he is the one who should be concerned with the effect of his work on people and the society they inhabit. On him depends, to a great extent, the satisfaction, the convenience and the delight that will be obtained from artifacts produced. He is required, by his professionalism, to take a wide view of both economy of production and the satisfaction of consumers. He is also in a favourable position to view the implications of his actions and be alert to the danger of creating new problems while solving others. As the man said when looking at a new motorway construction, 'I wonder which bottle-neck that leads to'.

Now these are big claims for any man to make and the best designers are suitably humble about their ability to cope with the demands of their profession. They tend to talk of 'modifying a situation' rather than 'solving a problem' since they know that, like perfection, a complete solution to many problems is unattainable. Yet the very demands made by their task elevate the role of a designer to a level that makes it a worthy basis on which to construct an educational system.

It might be well at this stage to consider why educationists at the present time seem so concerned to form new curriculum areas and to organize interdisciplinary studies. At one time in grammar schools one 'subject', the classics, was studied. This concentration on the one subject was not as narrow as might be imagined since, through the study of the writings of ancient times about our forebears' struggle to comprehend mankind and his world, pupils were led, themselves, to a broad understanding of the nature of man.

Gradually, as the sheer volume of knowledge accumulated, it became impossible for any one person – or certainly enough of them to staff our schools – to possess a broad understanding of the whole sweep of knowledge. Hence it became necessary to divide knowledge up into 'subjects' each of which was taught, in isolation, by different 'specialists'. Children were left to make their own integration and only the wisest managed to achieve an understanding that could relate one area of knowledge with another. The situation was made worse because the most intelligent were channelled into the narrowest of specialisms so that they could acquire such knowledge that they could still further extend the boundaries in their own specialism. Educationists are now aware of the need for understanding the interrelationship between different branches of knowledge; hence the setting up of interdisciplinary courses.

Design education is, therefore, an element in a general movement in education and has sound educational theory to support it. But the argument for design education does not rest only on a general idea that interdisciplinary studies are a good thing: it is a response to changes that are taking place in society as a whole. Although it is absurd to believe that because a thing has been done for many years it is, inevitably, wrong; it is equally absurd to assume it must be right and should remain unquestioned. We live in a time of unprecedented change and all of us must consider whether what we are doing is still appropriate to our present society.

If we are to develop an educational system that does take account of change then we must be clear in our minds about the nature of changes that are taking place. To do that thoroughly is a big task but some changes can be mentioned that have a particular bearing on practical education. They are the ones that are effected by increases of size and power in industry and government.

The increase in population and the development of world wide markets has led to mass production, automation and ever increasing size of industrial units. It is only by using all these aids to increased production that the basic needs of mankind can be satisfied. Large scale production is essential in this situation and is not necessarily a bad thing, but it does need a mass market and hence large numbers of people who will buy the same thing. There is a premium on conformity and a reduction in individuality. In a more crowded world there must be greater restriction on people's individual freedom or one person's freedom becomes another's restriction: what is a permissible level of noise in an isolated house becomes intolerable in a block of flats. So, in government, there is an increasing necessity to control individuals in the interests of society as a whole. What might have been a harmless and amusing eccentricity in an earlier age can now become a menace to others. In any case we have become more egalitarian so that extreme variations of wealth and poverty are no longer acceptable to us.

Another development that has had a profound effect on society has been the greater availability of energy. The unaided efforts of muscle power were unable to affect the landscape — the whole environment — to the extent of radical change. This is no longer true: quarrying, road construction, management of water, afforestation and deforestation can now take place on a scale that affects very considerably the visual and climatic conditions under which people live. No longer can this be left to individual decisions but society, as a whole, through Town and Country Planning Acts, has to take control.

All these changes have one thing in common: decisions that affect very large numbers have to be taken and these decisions are taken by bodies and individuals that, because of the numbers involved, are remote from those affected. There may well be more choice of goods, more choice of entertainment, more choice of food as a result of developments in industry, transport and communications, but it is a choice from what is available. If an individual has a particular and individual need that is not met by existing commerce then there is little chance of his getting it. The small unit that will produce for an individual order is very rare indeed, and if it exists is extremely expensive.

The danger of such developments is that we are reduced to conforming to a system we do not control and over which we have little influence. Market research only establishes what a sufficient number will accept; not what a significant number want. What becomes important is not consumer satisfaction but consumer acceptance.

A parallel situation in government exists in which 'they' take the decisions and 'we' can merely grumble impotently. The most likely reaction is apathy which leads directly to a slave state of dull acquiescence or, alternatively, to a violent rejection of society. It is only too easy to see evidence of both of these reactions in our society today. It is difficult to see how ordinary citizens can participate in the decisions that are taken in their name and many do not want to bother. It is certain that often the experts do know best, and decisions open to the influence of all people could well be worse by any objective standard. But the only hope of developing a lively, involved, caring society is to get people, as a whole, thinking in terms of 'our' decisions rather than 'their' decisions, and 'our' responsibility for our own society and its environment. Society has a long way to go if this willingness to be involved in decision-making is to become general. If the decisions taken are to be sound and realistic then the task is formidable.

As a good egalitarian I am distressed to note that all the nicest villages belong to one 'squire' who insists on taking personal responsibility for the construction and maintenance of 'his' village. Most of us, put in such a position, would display the same sort of responsibility. What we do not find so easy to do is to take responsibility, through our representatives, for the beauty and the tidiness of our town or city. We do not even approve if money is 'wasted' on making our environment more beautiful with flowers on traffic islands and lamp posts. The state of many of our cities bears witness to the peril of refusing such responsibility.

If people are to become so involved then they will have to develop a greater sensitivity to their material surroundings. They will have to understand far more of the nature of designing; the balancing of constraints so that the situation can be modified in a way that is not only most satisfying but sufficiently economical as to be feasible. In other words: in order to function as participating citizens in today's society, an understanding of design is essential, and so this must be included in any sound education.

This is the compelling argument for the establishing of design education: that it is a response by teachers to the challenge of change. It is their way of trying to do more to help their pupils cope with the role society is demanding of them. It would be unfair and stupid to expect craft teachers to take sole responsibility for this task but they must, if they are truly professional, ask themselves if they are doing all they can in this way. Because of the interest of pupils in workshop activities (established statistically in 'Survey One'), and because of the teachers' own skill in handling materials, and because they have the equipment available in their workshops, they have a golden opportunity to make a significant contribution. If this opportunity is neglected then they are depriving their pupils of help that is badly needed.

We have moved a long way since it was still possible for some teachers to maintain that children cannot design. A lot is owed to the pioneers who showed just what could be done. By now it is no longer open to question that there is a wide range of activities that can be organized in schools that lead a pupil to the stage where he can sustain, credibly, the role of a designer. It is fascinating to see how closely these developments parallel developments in educational theory.

Some research at the Royal College of Art gives the clue as to why this is. Attempts there were made to define the activity of designing. The idea of a 'design line' whereby decision follows decision with ruthless logic is now known to be inaccurate. Feed-back, circular thinking, even mosaic thinking were shown to be engaged in by practising designers so that it proved extremely difficult to set down any model on which the process could be based. Then two separate pieces of research intersected and, as shown by Professor Bruce Archer, it became apparent that the designing process is very similar to the learning process.

If we look at the designing process within education we immediately come across parallels. Design work must be 'child-centred' since it is nothing if not individual. All children may be put into the same situation and subjected to the same constraints of time, materials and facilities for working them, but unless they are free to produce their own response to that situation then they are not designing.

Because designing can take place, at their own level, in such a way that they can actually realize their designs in real material for a real purpose, the work is a 'genuine first hand experience' — not as in so much school work, bookish and second-hand. Moreover it is 'relevant' to the child, his experience and his own personal environment. He can, literally, by producing something he needs or wants, modify his own situation. This can be done with 'success at different levels' because there is never one solution to a problem but any number of possibilities. These can be of widely differing sophistication. To quote a simple example already used elsewhere: two bricks wrapped in decorative paper and an elaborate bookcase are both legitimate solutions to the problem of keeping a collection of books tidy. One is so simple that there is hardly a pupil who could be incapable of tackling it, while the other could fully extend the most accomplished craftsman. In doing so the interest of both would be maintained which would not be the case if all were expected to work at the same level, since that would outface one and bore the other.

There has been a tendency by society to keep thinking and feeling apart. The harsh division at sixth form level in many schools between the arts and the sciences is one evidence of this, and the division persists in the universities. There is far too great a tendency to regard the arts as a gloss on life and to turn only to the sciences when planning a course of action. This is exaggerated because the arguments of the sciences can be stated in quantitative terms — 'that will add 50p per square foot to the cost of the building' — whereas the qualitative arguments of the arts are only expressed in terms of opinions. Yet decisions taken purely on quantitative assessments can often, in retrospect, be shown to be unwise: the closing of socially desirable branch railway lines and the building of socially undesirable high-rise flats are cases of this.

Designing is, above all, the activity that uses and unites both feeling and thinking. A successful designer must have a feeling for qualities and a sound knowledge of the scientific thinking on which production and economics are based. Hence designing is an excellent way of bridging the gap and encouraging pupils, naturally, to use both

14

sensitivity and intelligence in making decisions. This is another sound reason for including it in general education.

These arguments for considering design as an essential element in general education seem to me to be compelling. There is no doubt that the activity is an ideal medium through which pupils can be helped to a broad understanding of their own society and environment. So much of our environment is man-made and formed by design decisions that some understanding of the way these decisions are made is essential for intelligent participation. Practically the whole of industry now produces goods that are the result of conscious design decisions; not a traditional development of something which has been produced by craftsmen down the centuries. Goods are not produced by tradesmen for their known customers but are turned out in factories remote from point of sale. A 'consumer revolution' may stop the sale of shoddy or dangerous goods, but if the quality of goods is to be improved then the criticism must be on a sufficiently informed level to take into account all the constraints of production and economy that operate.

The aims set forth are high and make great demands on teachers who seek to attain them. It is not surprising that some have not been very successful. It is particularly unfortunate that those who wish for an excuse to avoid uncomfortable change can point to the failures and ask if the new is worse than the old. But it is quite wrong to condemn a plan of education because some practitioners are unsuccessful — otherwise all schools would have to close. Criticism of the way people introduce design education and the methods they use is sometimes taken to be criticism of the principle of design education. The 'materials circus' and the 'connecting theme' — both legitimate enough if well done — can, when ineptly handled, lead to work that is unrealistic and a waste of the precious expertise of the teacher and the equipment at his disposal.

No teacher should be asked to work in a way that he himself finds unconvincing — and indeed this should not be necessary. All forms of practical work, the workshop crafts included, already embrace, traditionally, many activities that are totally relevant to good design education. So often it is a question of change of approach and attitude to the work and the pupil rather than a change in the actual work done. Design education can be and should be a development that naturally arises out of the work that has gone before. It is a way of making craft activities more relevant to the condition of the pupils and the society in which they live. The introduction of design education should not be in conflict with the past and it should not offend the crafts teacher who genuinely wants to help his pupils to the best of his ability.

The only way to test the truth of this claim is to write down a list of the reasons why crafts are taught in schools. Clearly the objective is not to turn out craftsmen, any more than art education should seek to turn everyone into an artist. Crafts teachers have never been content merely to train their pupils in a skill. As long ago as the twenties of this century it was said that we were less concerned with the effect of the boy on the wood than the effect of the wood on the boy. Otherwise it was believed that learning to be a craftsman had some influence on the personal development of the pupil.

What was forgotten was that becoming a craftsman was so demanding that few attained that level and so reaped the full benefit from the training given. Yet in today's world when most people are so remote from primary production and so many live artificial urban lives is there not an even greater need for the contact with reality that comes of craft activity? I would submit, therefore, that one of the more important aims of craft education is to provide that contact: to give the opportunity for pupils to gain an interest in and respect for materials. If such an attitude could be developed it would be a major antidote to planned obsolescence and the throw-away society that bids fair to despoil the world and waste our stocks of scarce resources.

It has always seemed to me that the constant call for decisions that is part of craftmanship is an admirable way of developing responsibility, so this would also appear in my personal list of reasons for teaching crafts. Once a piece of material is cut it can never be returned, exactly, to its former state. If it is cut in the wrong place no power on earth will make it fit the purpose intended, but the craftsman must have the courage to back his judgment. The demand to make decisions of this sort — and stand by the result — calls for, and gives opportunities for the development of, the best sort of responsibility. No one can develop this respect for materials and this concern for the result of one's decisions without developing a sense of fitness of things. If time, effort, skill, and the cost of materials, are to be used in producing something then it must be good or the time, effort, skill and materials are wasted. There must be a different attitude towards something produced personally in this way than towards something acquired for mere money.

More than most does the craftsman have opportunities to visualize things not yet made. He must be quite clear about the final form of his work before he starts shaping material to make it. This ability to foresee the result of actions is a most valuable quality and one that is all too rare. It is not impossible to find highly intelligent and educated people who, apparently, do not possess it to any degree at all.

It would be possible to add to this list, and I would suggest this as a valuable exercise for all teachers. Possibly the ones I have selected will be adequate to make the point. All the qualities that I have suggested are encouraged by crafts education are essential to good designing and must therefore be equally encouraged by design education. To return to an earlier point, if we will only consider why we teach, rather than how we teach, then any apparent conflict between craft education and design education disappears.

I have suggested that today individuals must be involved in the decisions made on their behalf: that they must participate. The same thing is true of teachers regarding decisions made by teachers about the organization of education in their schools, and specifically by teachers of practical subjects when design departments are set up. Craft teachers have so much to offer and can make a very positive contribution. If they do take a positive attitude then their contribution will not be overlooked and the work that will evolve will not run contrary to what they feel to be right. The converse is also unfortunately true and if their attitude is negative and unco-operative then they cannot sensibly protest if, without their help, work evolves in a way that they believe is wrong.

There is so much to be gained for the crafts by the development of good design education that the effort is well worth while. Many crafts teachers still feel that their work lacks recognition and that its status is low. It should and can play a far more central role in education. Design education seeks, by elevating those aspects which most clearly bear on the understanding of man and his environment, to establish the central role of all practical subjects. By doing this it does not diminish the importance of craft education but greatly enhances it.

This is not just hopeful theory. I, personally, have seen the improvement of status that takes place where successful design departments have been established. The head of such a department, who could well be a crafts teacher, not only has status (and salary) commensurate with his position, but he can, because he is the head of one of the biggest and most important departments in the school, speak for the importance of practical work when school policy is being discussed. He can, and must be able to, advance the arguments that we have all known but have found difficulty in getting accepted. This is a very real gain and revolutionizes the attitude of educationists to the importance of the crafts in an education that is relevant today.

16

3

Structuring a basic design course
An analysis of the course at Pocklington School
R.N. BILLINGTON AND J.R. JEFFERY

Nigel Billington and John R Jeffery are jointly in charge of the Design Centre at Pocklington School. Nigel Billington was trained as a designer at the then Manchester Regional College of Art and has taught at Pocklington for the past sixteen years. During this time he has had an increasing interest in preparing boys for professional careers in architecture and industrial design. John Jeffery has a degree in electrical engineering and worked in the telecommunications industry for four years. He taught physics before taking up his present post in 1969.

Abstract   This paper describes the organization of a design course for boys aged between eleven and thirteen years. It covers the integration of imaginative, intuitive, technical and aesthetic concepts as well as the teaching strategy employed.

Introduction

Pocklington School is an independent boys' day boarding school. The Design and Creation Centre, which opened in January 1970, brought together under one roof an existing art department and a new technical unit. From the outset it was decided that the Centre should develop an integrated approach rather than separate art and technical courses and this has led to the development of a basic course which aims to challenge a boy's intelligence and appeal to his creative and aesthetic instincts. The course as developed at present is followed by all boys in the eleven-plus to thirteen-plus age range. (There are approximately sixty to eighty boys in each year group).

All boys in Forms I, II and III are timetabled to spend two double periods each week in the Centre, one on the art side and the other on the technical. This distribution varies from time to time and a group may spend all four periods in one place, or two groups may be combined together for a joint session if a particular phase of their work demands it. In the IVth form boys may opt to take art as an O level subject and continue on to A level in the VIth form. There are no examinations at present in craft or technical drawing, although technical projects are offered as part of the VIth form general studies programme. There are, however, plans to extend the present three year integrated design course through to VIth form level with examinations at O and A level.

The Design Centre is situated in a new single-storey prefabricated building with an H-shaped open-plan arrangement of seven main teaching areas as shown in fig. 1, and has a total ground area of 6,750 square feet. In all the early planning of the enterprise there was the fullest possible consultation between the school's architect and ourselves, which has allowed us to have complete control of the ground plan, provision and lay out of services, design of furniture and fittings, and selection of equipment. This freedom has resulted in a building that has yet to limit our activities, although in our work we naturally concentrate on a fewer number of activities at any moment than would be possible in a large design complex. However, we do not feel that this is particularly disadvantageous.

The decision to integrate the main outline of the work has demanded a close collaboration between the teaching staff. Naturally, the greater the number of people involved in a particular scheme, the greater the difficulties involved in ensuring common objectives and the co-ordinated activity that enables a single piece of work to be pursued in a number of different areas. In the light of our experience with part-time teachers, students, and schemes with local art and teacher training colleges we feel that the problem of scale is of vital importance in the success of a design department.

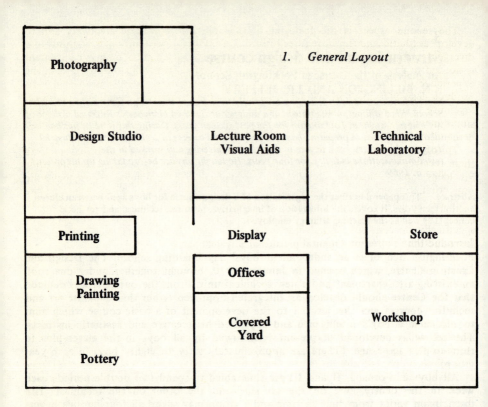

Photography

Design Studio

Lecture Room
Visual Aids

Technical
Laboratory

Printing

Display

Store

Drawing
Painting

Offices

Covered
Yard

Workshop

Pottery

What we may lose in extensive facilities is more than compensated for by increased cohesion within the unit.

The approach to design education

Fundamentally we aim to provide a properly and excitingly structured, widely based course that gives a strong impulse to creative design but is at the same time appropriately geared to the age and experience of the children. We believe that both structure and external discipline are necessary in any course for children of this age. Children react readily to attractive stimuli and we try to build on the child's interests, not in a way that capitulates to the child, but rather in a sensitive way that extends him, for at this age he is not necessarily the best judge of his own development. However, having said this, whenever a particular child shows strongly developed personal ideas (either emotional or intellectual) we naturally encourage them enthusiastically.

The first requirement in the development of design awareness is a strong emphasis on the knowledge and understanding achieved through the study and analysis of natural and man-made forms which stimulates both the intellect and the imagination. The child discovers through these exercises (in drawing, painting and modelling) how things look, feel, work and behave. The various approaches possible in these exercises, such as observational, analytical and conceptual drawing, greatly enlarge the child's experience of the structural, technical and aesthetic qualities in the world around him. These experiences will also, taken as a whole, stimulate in him a feeling for the quality of organic vitality and growth. We call this gaining of experience the process of 'data gathering', and believe it to be of the first importance to the development of design awareness.

The second aspect is the fostering of the ability to speculate creatively and to develop aesthetic and emotional responses. This ability to extemporize or think in a divergent manner is at the root of artistic creativity and a similar mental excitement is needed to spark off ideas in the technical and craft fields. Thus, building from the experience of the 'data gathering' stage, a child progressively develops an ability to produce designs to meet all manner of given or self-motivated specifications. Technical ingenuity is successfully fostered in children of this age through posing problems that simultaneously excite the sense of form and structure, contain a technical element and demand practical realization.

Thirdly, the generation of creative ideas can only be effective if the ability to express them receives equal attention. From the outset of the course a pupil learns to express his ideas rapidly through sketches and drawings. The principles of orthographic projection, for example, are used when workshop drawings are needed, although the emphasis is always on conveying the necessary information quickly and accurately rather than on formal drawing techniques. On the practical side, it is important to specifically develop conceptual drawing skills, by which we mean the ability to first form and then represent a mental picture of physical parts.

In many situations a workshop drawing is not feasible or appropriate and a three-dimensional mock-up is the only way in which an individual's ideas can be adequately expressed. The emphasis in the first mock-up must be presentation of the basic idea for subsequent individual or group comment and rationalization. It is after this stage that the practical details of materials and craft processes need to be considered; specific demonstrations and exercises may be necessary. The choice of modelling material will certainly influence the design, and wherever possible the scale of the mock-up should be that of the final product.

Technical concepts are initially treated intuitively but as the course proceeds they are developed in greater detail by structured exercises that concentrate on a qualitative understanding of key ideas with the minimum (or no) quantitative material. In order to maintain spontaneity and the flow of further creative ideas during the workshop stage it is important that a design is not exhaustively developed or over finished as a mock-up. We realize that this approach differs from adult design practice but in a school the workshop is as much a learning and experimental situation as a production unit.

This sequential and ordered series of art, technical and craft experience has meant that each subject is considered not so much as a self-contained body of knowledge and experience, but more as a flexible tool to the other in assisting the total learning experience of the child. When suitably stimulated a child is enthusiastically ready to acquire the skills and techniques needed to achieve the creative ends he has in mind, whether it is an illustration, a pot, a tile panel, or a mechanical toy, and will be prepared to take them to the highest standards of which he is capable.

Overall, a pupil needs a disciplined and ordered series of experiences. His imagination must be fed by direct observational drawing, which should be followed by analytical studies to deepen his intuitive awareness of colour, texture, structural and mechanical form. It is from these sources that his subsequent ideas will grow. He will need periods of craft instruction and the experience of working with materials. Technical problems must be analyzed in the same way, treating the underlying concepts in an intuitive and qualitative manner. It is vital that the work maintains its excitement at every stage, for the richest learning experiences occur when the structural, technical and aesthetic factors act simultaneously as complementary parts of the total situation[1].

The following section contains an outline of the three-year scheme of work. As with any developing scheme, ideas change rapidly in the light of experience and particular topics are introduced or modified as the response to them by the children, and our insight into them, is gauged.

Outline of the three-year scheme of work

PROJECT 1 (YEAR 1)

Art side	*Technical side*
1a Free exploration of pattern through shape, colour and surface quality.	**1b** Exploration of geometrically based pattern through templates and drawing instruments.

2 General discussion of work from both sources. Comparison with examples from Islamic architecture and natural sources. Discussion of other ways of producing pattern; the emergence of the concept of *interlocking* and *interslotting* as the basis of design.

3a Introduction of natural forms as a pattern source: analysis of shape and pattern and their development into a working drawing for coping saw exercise.	**3b** Preliminary workshop exercise based on an element from 3a. Introduction to the idea of a trial run.
4a Further imaginative development of 3a into a three-dimensional object, e.g. as a mobile or kite. Discussion and experiment with structure, shape, material and colour.	**4b** Manufacture of interlocking/interslotting design produced at 3a. Introduction to craft aspect of 'waste wood', and 'waste side of the line'.
5a Drawing and painting work, more emotionally based, but developing above concepts further. Final decoration of 5b here, or at a later date.	**5b** Assembly of pattern into frame and backing. Simple finishing (see 5a).

PROJECT 2 (YEAR 1)

Art and Technical side combined

FIRST METALWORK AND MECHANICAL EXERCISE containing elements of rotating/sliding parts; pivots; suspension or steering; and if possible string or rubber band operation.

1 Stimulus material, e.g. films, slides, or displays around themes such as war machines, grabs, cranes, moon vehicles or science fiction (Dr Who) situations.

2 First mock-up giving a rapid statement of ideas in durable, but easily worked materials.

3 Class discussion session to establish the direction of future work and elicit the mechanical aspects, importance of scale, and the constructional/craft aspects needed in taking the work further.

4 Development and recording of designs through sketches and part mock-ups of mechanical or craft aspects. N.B. This is the stage at which a design can become too finalized, thus inhibiting further natural and spontaneous development in the workshop.

Art side	*Technical side*
5a Introduction to the study of human form – proportion, structure, positions, situations. Working from imagination after this stimulation: extemporizing, e.g. fantastic figures in fantastic landscapes. Imaginative use of paint and graphic media.	**5b** Workshop fabrication, covering the processes of marking out, fitting, drilling, bending, forming, jointing and finishing.

PROJECT 3 (YEAR 1)
WOODEN TOTEM: WOODWORK AND DECORATION EXERCISE

Art side	*Technical side*
1a Study of stimulus for 'totem' design; use of blocks to help visualize design on paper in felt pen (as face and edge views). Immediate excitement of decorative possibilities.	Project 2 stage 5b being completed in workshop at this time.
2a Design of a more symbolic totem.	**2b** Development of face and edge views from 1a. Need to resolve design in terms of given timber. Preparatory craft exercise.
3a Further developments to design, e.g. for carving in wood or plaster, theatrical costumes, etc.	**3b** Workshop production of totem, covering marking out and most joint cutting techniques. (Prepared timber used for speed).

4 Alternative approach to totem, e.g. freer carved forms and a more sensitive working of the material.

PROJECT 4 (YEAR 2)

Art side

1a Analytical drawing of fruit, flowers etc. leading towards stylized designs.

2a Production of design for enamelled or etched medallion; developed to the stage of a card and wire mock-up.

3a Figure drawing: analytical approach, basic movements, proportion, posture, contraposto. Further more emotionally based work, drawing of wrestling and intertwining figures: restatement of the concept of interslotting and interlocking.

4a Possible further development of 2a into small scale wire and membrane (scrim, tissue/dope) model. Stress placed on retaining the intrinsic qualities of the original fruit; and the possibility of further embellishment.

Technical side

1b First conceptual drawing exercise involving the directed-sketching of simple geometric forms.

2b Demonstration of enamelling or etching and associated metal work techniques.

2c Wire soldering exercise to develop sensitivity of touch and experience of working at a jewellery scale. Incorporating material from 1a.

3b Execution of medallion designs from 2a.

PROJECT 5 (YEAR 2)

Art side

1a Conceptual drawing; from memory, from verbal description. Simple introduction to basic perspective, movement through space. Indoor and outdoor sketching; atmosphere and mood. From mood to dramatic situations.

2a Sketchbook and scrapbooks: data gathering through the recording of information of all kinds.

3a Finishing of interpenetrating block exercise from 2b as a simple colour exercise.

Technical side

1b Further conceptual drawing leading on from Project 4, 1b, to slotting, sliding and mechanical movements. Development in terms of interpenetrating blocks through a series of sketches. Introduction of the concept of orthographic projection.

2b Woodworking exercise: production of designs from 2b. Practical limitations imposed by available materials: production of workshop drawing (squared paper).
Execution in workshop; basic processes of timber preparation and working. Simple finishing.

PROJECT 6 (YEAR 2)

Art side

1a Discussion of polyester resin techniques and the preparation of a suitable design from drawing of plants and figures.

2a Execution of polyester resin mat or panel. Affinity with stained glass, or alternative mosaic design.

Technical side

1b Introduction to the properties of plastic materials through film, slides, and simple physical tests.

2b Working with plastics, designs involving bending and forming of thermoplastic sheet. Alternatively, the production of cast or embedded items.

21

3b Metalwork exercise: to widen experience of craft processes through the production of small tools, e.g. screwdriver, pin hammer, fishing equipment.

PROJECT 7 (YEAR 3)

At the beginning of the third year there is a Common Entrance intake to the School producing four forms instead of two. Each set of two forms comes to the Centre for double period sessions twice a week. They are usually divided into three classes – pottery; workshop and technical work; drawing, painting and analytical work – spending about a term on each activity. However, greater freedom of choice is given to boys at this stage to choose which activity they wish to follow. The year's work starts with a design and a technical exercise during the first two weeks, which is used in a diagnostic sense to assist in the choice of options during the remainder of the year:

Art side	*Technical side*
Containing form exercise in light card based on drawings and diagrams of ovaries, kernels, fruit etc. Over the two sessions it emerges that the repetition and interlocking of similar shapes give rise to the most satisfying forms.	Simple structures exercise designed to give a qualitative understanding of the properties of tensile and compressive members in a structure through experiments with straw and thread. Testing (to destruction) of all designs: goodness and relative performance.

During the third year a boy may be involved in any of the following activities, depending on his own choice:

Art side

(i) Drawing, painting and graphics,
Introduction to subject of composition, through study of historically important painters.
Preparation of a composition, collection of 'data' and numerous sketches.
Emergence and crystallizing of an idea: paint quality and experiments with various media.

(ii) Pottery: form and decoration, slab and coil techniques, surface treatment and quality. Tiles, pressed dishes and the possibility of group projects.
(iii) Other possibilities include screen printing, batik, polyester resin forms, decorative panels and table tops.

Technical side

(i) Combined art/workshop/technical project, arising from a further study of stimulus material (e.g. insect or animal form) and leading to articulated model in card or other materials. Investigation and development of appropriate technical aspects of the design, e.g. linkage or other mechanism. Combination in the workshop of the work from both the above stages to produce the final model.
(ii) Technical investigation into structures with further qualitative experiments with sheet structures. Final design/build problem.

(iii) Technical investigation into the performance of simple gliders (stability, lift, etc.) through the construction of various wing configurations. Final design/development problem, e.g. the incorporation of rubber powered propeller.
(iv) Introduction of casting, e.g. to a screen wall brief or interlocking vertebrae structure.
(v) Craft work, the production of a wide variety of artifacts to the highest personal standards, e.g. veneered or painted boxes, beaten metalwork, turned bowls, tables, carving.

Notes and References

1 The integration that has been achieved in this course between art, craft and technology has been described in 'Studies in Design Education and Craft', Vol. 5, No. 2, 1973, and in *School Technology in Action* by A.R. Marshall, English University Press & Open University (1974).

4

Design: where does it start and where does it end?

J. CLAY

John Clay is Senior Lecturer at Crewe and Alsager College of Higher Education responsible for academic coordination within the Faculty of Creative Arts. He is leader of a team presenting proposals for the establishment of a BA degree in Design in Society. He is a graduate of the Open University, has wide experience of teaching in schools and is a consultant designer to the furniture and plastics industries.

Abstract   This paper suggests a clarification of the definition of design following an isolation and interpretation of the component features. It demonstrates in diagrammatic form both the linearity of the contributory parts and their hierarchical aspects. It emphasizes the universitality of the breadth of the process of design education and points to a solution in unification.

Much of the argument about design stems, not from the philosophy or process of design, but from the different conceptions of what it is and what it should be concerned with. Whilst many have attempted a form of words to define design, from the systematic 'a goal-directed, problem-solving activity' (L. Bruce Archer) to the rather light-hearted 'performing a very complicated act of faith' (J. Christopher Jones), it is in the interpretation of these words that very real differences occur. Therefore any design conference should address itself to the problem of definition, not necessarily to resolve the issue, but to reveal the attitudes and assumptions of those present about this central issue, so that in later discussions each person is more aware of the interpretation of the term used by each of the others.

I have quoted two definitions, there are many others: 'relating product with situation to give satisfaction' (Gregory) and 'the imaginative jump from present facts to future possibilities' (Page) are two. Popularly design is associated with the production of artifacts as in furniture or engineering design, however, one can equally speak of designing a strategy or designing a syllabus. There is indeed hardly any field of human activity in which the term design is not used.

The main recurring theme in all these diverse definitions and uses of the term is that an activity is taking place, the activity of designing. One may consider this a trite observation but it does draw attention to the idea that to understand design one must examine not 'designs' but 'designing'. Whilst this is not a new idea it is by no means universally accepted. Indeed the idea of teaching people to appreciate 'good' design is built on teaching an understanding of design through the study of designs. I suggest that the concept of 'good' design is unhelpful to an examination of designing for is 'good' to be judged against some sort of standard such as might be used when deciding on a design award? Or is it to be a measure of value to the community? Or a measure of extent to which a client's requirements have been met? The debate about 'good' and 'bad' design draws attention to the end result and away from the activity unless in an attempt to define 'good' the process is examined.

Designing is initiated by a problem, often stated in the form of a brief, and this is usually taken as the starting point of a sequence of activities following the form of diagram 1.

However, the brief is the outcome of another, previous design activity. Take for example the brief to design a bathroom, this could be the outcome of designing a modular housing system and it is also likely to produce the brief for the design of a wash basin thus coming in the middle of a hierarchy of design problems such as that in diagram 2.

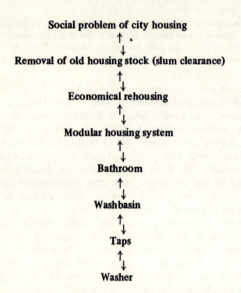

Analysis of the problem

↓

Generation and development of ideas

↓

Selection, by evaluation, of a preferred solution

Diagram 1

Social problem of city housing

↑ ↓

Removal of old housing stock (slum clearance)

↑ ↓

Economical rehousing

↑ ↓

Modular housing system

↑ ↓

Bathroom

↑ ↓

Washbasin

↑ ↓

Taps

↑ ↓

Washer

Diagram 2 (The use of names, − bathroom taps etc., − can disguise the problem, they are used here for convenience.)

It is in this hierarchy that the differences in definitions are most pronounced. Most people would accept that designing a bathroom or washbasin, or even the taps and the housing system, is designing as an artifact is produced and its appearance is important, thereby taking the general view that design is to do with the appearance of artifacts. Somehow designing a washer does not have the same immediate recognition as a design activity but nevertheless would be accepted as such by most designers, as would designing an economical rehousing system. But how often is the problem of slum clearance or even less the social problems of city housing considered to be a design problem?

But the problems are so interconnected that decisions taken at one point in the hierarchy affect decisions at other points. For instance, a decision about slum clearance policy can substantially affect the ability to solve the social problems of city housing. How often is the design of a wash basin controlled by the design of the taps, and the bathroom by the wash basin, and so on, so that in the end the problems of city centre housing are affected by the design of a washer? So at least on the grounds of inter-

24

connection there is no case for considering designing at different points in the hierarchy as separate activities. Nor is there a case for separation on the grounds that the process is different at different points.

It hardly needs illustration that the process at each stage fits both the definitions and the outline process of analysis, generation, development and selection given earlier but the similarity persists in the details. The analysis of the problem in each case will involve the investigation of human, economic, environment and technical factors. The investigation of human behaviour and expectations is as important in the design of a bathroom as it is in considering the problems of city housing. The techniques of observation and interview used to collect the relevant data are often the same. The same can be said of economic and environmental concepts and technique. It is only in the technical factors that a difference may be observed. The technicalities of designing a tap may well be different from those of designing a system of housing but even these are related, for instance the type of mixer tap used in a shower is affected by the positioning of the header tank in the hot water system, so the technical problems of one are also the technical problems of the other. Furthermore, the techniques of production are related to the sociology of the means of production.

At the stage of generating ideas the technique of synectics is specifically based on bringing together people with backgrounds in different disciplines in order that, for instance, a problem of traffic flow may be considered by, say, a heating engineer concerned with hot air and water flows or a biologist concerned with flows in the body. One might indeed say that most technical innovation is the result of using an established principle in a new context. The principle of support on jets of air, or water, was well known before the hovercraft, the innovation was to use it in transport. Thus at the synthesis stage the boundaries of design are not fixed any more than during the problem analysis, and in fact the fixing of a false boundary can inhibit the generation of a solution.

The implementation of the solution, or even its proposal, affects the problem which originated the activity, (the game 'Delphi' attempts to simulate this) and also other problems in the hierarchy. Hence the diagrams of the design activity could be revised to look like diagram 3.

Designing is a complex activity and to understand it one must understand the complexity. I have argued that it is in this understanding that design in all fields converge, and further that to confine the study of design to one field is to neglect the essential complex nature of design and thus not understand it.

The implications of this argument for design in general and design education in particular are extensive but I would point to three main conclusions:

1 that the appreciation of design is the appreciation of the problem and the environment within which it is situated

2 that design should be concerned with those problems and aspects of problems for which the likely end product may not be an artifact as much as those which are. In fact to do nothing could be a legitimate solution to a design problem

3 that the education of those intending to operate in any fields of design should be equally concerned with an understanding of the language and methods of those involved with the whole design problem as with the technicalities of a particular specialized sector.

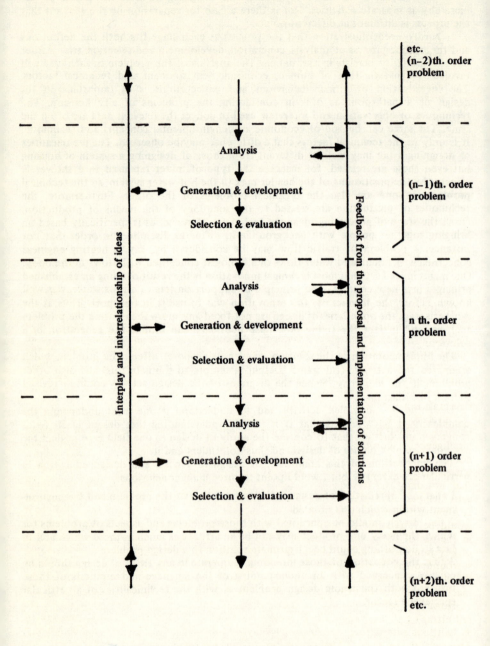

etc.
(n−2)th. order
problem

Analysis

Generation & development

Selection & evaluation

(n−1)th. order
problem

Analysis

Generation & development

Selection & evaluation

n th. order
problem

Analysis

Generation & development

Selection & evaluation

(n+1) order
problem

Feedback from the proposal and implementation of solutions

Interplay and interrelationship of ideas

(n+2)th. order
problem
etc.

3 A small section of the design activity

5
Epistemological issues and the status of craftwork
R. T. CRYER

Roger T. Cryer teaches at Millfield where he has developed a unique system of audio-visual presentation for craft and design teaching. He is currently researching at Bristol University.

Abstract   This paper is part of an extended thesis on the Philosophy of Craft Education registered at the University of Bristol. Other essays within the thesis explore historical and moral issues. Here it is argued that 'craft' is not a mechanical art. Established concepts are questioned and the interrelationship between ideas, the emotions and evaluative considerations are explored and discussed. The significance of the paper is such that it provides a philosophy which has governed the development and use of closed-circuit television and audio-visual programmed learning in a school workshop.

The following quotation taken from D'Alembert's writings provides the essence of our first problem:

> But as there are rules for the operation of the mind and soul, so are there rules for the operation of the body; that is to say, for those operations which limited to exterior objects are worked solely by the force of arm. Hence the distinction of liberal arts (fine arts) and mechanical arts (crafts) and the superiority accorded to the former over the latter.[1]

There are difficulties here for the evaluative statement which accords superiority to the liberal arts as it is derived from a factual statement. Thus D'Alembert derives an 'ought' from an 'is', or in other words an evaluation from a fact. The validity of the argument cannot therefore be upheld for an evaluation is introduced in the conclusion which is not contained in the original premise. However the central thesis of this essay is not concerned with the logical validity of the quotation, but rather with the notion that craft is a 'mechanical art'.

Our task is to argue that craft is not a 'mechanical art'. For reasons which will become evident in the following argument, mechanical is taken to mean 'without intelligence or conscious will performed simply by the force of habit'.[2] But it will not be denied that craft involves machines or mechanisms and is mechanical in this sense. Neither will it be denied that craft involves the use of the hand. Furthermore we shall not deny that there is a valid distinction between mechanical or habitual human activities and its antonym non-mechanical activities. We are then contending against D'Alembert's usage of the term mechanical to describe 'craft'. Indeed if we did not it would be impossible to fulfil the three criteria which have been accepted as implicit in the use of the word 'education'. The issue of mechanical versus non-mechanical is of key importance, indeed it is a recurring feature of the unceasing debate which has surrounded the development of craft education. That it was manifested in the era of William Morris, albeit in those days as a dispute of hand craftsmanship against the machine, demonstrates the ubiquity of the issue.

However, before progressing any further we must clarify the position we are criticizing by illustrating how in D'Alembert's writings 'mechanical' must be interpreted as 'without intelligence or conscious will performed simply by the force of habit'.[2] The central point in D'Alembert's distinction between 'liberal' and 'mechanical' arts is that 'mechanical' arts are governed exclusively by bodily actions whilst 'liberal' arts are controlled by the mind. D'Alembert does of course accept it is a prejudicial view which accords superiority to the 'liberal' arts and he attempts to explain its origin in sociological terms. But this explanation, while being plausible, implicitly accepts the original distinction between, 'the rules for the operation of the mind and soul and the rules for the operation of the body'. It therefore follows that if we are to dispute that craft is a mechanical art we have to dispute D'Alembert's first premise.

The heart of our problem is then the distinction between, 'rules for the operation of the mind and soul and rules for the operation of the body'. This distinction between mind and body is a belief deeply entrenched in the major European philosophical tradition. Basically this conception, although it has been compiled in more and more sophisticated forms throughout history holds that man consists of two substances, mental and material. However, our chief concern is to confine attention to a particular aspect of this theory, by concentrating on the term 'mechanical' in relation to that theory rather than expounding its philosophical history. By employing this tactic not only do we expose the assumption behind the notion that craft is a mechanical activity, we also relate this assumption to Galileo and Descartes. What then was Galileo's view?

> The forces in the sky are of the same kind as those on earth, that is what Galileo asserts; so that mechanical experiments that we perform here give us information about the stars. By turning his telescope on the moon, on Jupiter and on the sunspots, he put an end to the classical belief that the heavens are perfect and unchanging and only the earth is subject to the laws of change.[3]

Galileo therefore showed 'that his methods of scientific discovery were competent to provide a mechanical theory which should cover every occupant of space'.[4] This scientific discovery had a profound effect upon Galileo's contemporary René Descartes, a man of scientific genius he was influenced by the claims of mechanical theory. But Descartes had arrived at a conception of himself as a thinking being without reference to physical facts and material substances. He therefore believed in the intrinsic independence of the mind from the body, though a special theory was provided to account for their apparent interaction.

> According to this theory we are constituted of two entities – the body which is a complicated mechanism or organism functioning according to ascertainable scientific laws and the mind which we are made aware of by introspection. These two entities somehow interact on each other.[5]

Thus we have the notion of matter, that is the body, manifested in bodily movements, existing in time and space and therefore being explained by the mechanical laws which also explain matter, wherever it is to be found in time and space. In the same way, the mind may be understood as a non-spatial entity governed by non-mechanical causes, which also explain other non-spatial entities. In some way these two entities interact on each other.

But what are the implications for craft in this view? For clearly such implications are our prime concern. A quotation from Ryle provides not only the answer to the question but also makes clear the view which we are rejecting. Moreover, Ryle's comments justify the interpretation of 'mechanical' asserted earlier.

> The difference between the human behaviours which we describe as intelligent and those which we describe as unintelligent must be a difference in their causation; so while some movements of human tongues and limbs are the effects of mechanical causes others must be the effects of non-mechanical causes, i.e. some issue from movements of matter, others from working of the mind.[6]

There is of course a further difficulty for whilst the doctrine 'maintains that there exist both bodies and minds; that there occur physical processes and mental processes'[7], it also accepts because of the interaction of the two entities 'that there are physical causes of corporeal movements and mental causes of corporeal movements'[7].

But D'Alembert's statement leaves us in no doubt that crafts are regarded as mechanical activities fulfilled solely through 'physical causes of corporeal movements', and do not involve 'mental causes of corporeal movements'. Hence 'minds are things but different sorts of things from bodies; mental processes are causes and effects, but different sorts of causes and effects from bodily movements'.[6]

Thus if 'craft' when defined as a 'mechanical' art is conceived as an activity which is controlled by physical causes of bodily movements and if such bodily movements are mechanical in the sense that they are activated by physical causes, it is hardly surprising that there arose the notion of 'crafts' being activities which did not demand the powers of the intellect.

In exposing the belief that 'craft' is a mechanical activity we have exposed a belief which is based on the doctrine of the 'Ghost in the Machine'. Hence the belief that craft is a mechanical activity is based on another belief which is deeply ingrained in mankind and has had a long philosophical history. Perhaps it is this belief which accounts for Dearden's view of crafts as 'domestic skills' and Peter's conception of pottery as 'mere know how or knack'. Moreover, such a belief explains why 'craft' has rarely attained parity with other subjects in academic institutions. For the duality doctrine subscribes to the rationalist theory that 'the sovereign method for getting knowledge is through pure thought, reason alone'.[8]

Therefore, in arguing that craft is not a 'mechanical art', we shall be arguing against the belief that the mind is something autonomous being disembodied and independent of biological and physical needs. We do not deny that there are physical causes of corporeal movements. But we do deny the mind is autonomous in the sense that it always functions independently of sense experience and bodily movements. As indeed did the philosophers of the empiricist tradition, for they never held that the mind does function independently of the body and sense experience.

Granted these assumptions we shall argue that craft is not a mechanical activity. This will be achieved not by replacing the doctrine of the 'Ghost in the Machine' with an alternative theory but by showing through the example of a craft skill, that craft necessarily involves mental causes of corporeal movements. Indeed we shall prove by this example that a skilled performance is impossible if corporeal movements are not governed by mental causes. Thus we shall seek to refute D'Alembert's first premise which culminates in the statement, 'that is to say for those operations which limited to exterior objects are worked solely by the force of arm'.[1]

The example we shall analyse is that of planing, for this process has frequently been classified as a mechanical or bodily movement, governed by physical causes. Let us assume that a young man has been taught the first principles of planing. He can distinguish between sharp and blunt planes. Moreover, he understands the theory of the cutting action and the way in which the plane iron should be sharpened and adjusted. Furthermore, he comprehends the concept of rectangularity and appreciates if he is to produce a cuboid of given dimensions, he must, at outset, plane a flat side. At this point, his teacher gives a very skilful demonstration of planing accompanied by a verbal descriptive account of the process. Our young man has now a complete grasp of the underlying principles, in addition he has witnessed the performance of the skill. Now, it seems purely a question of bodily movements. The young man proceeds with his task but fails to produce a flat side on his timber, indeed we will assume that he produces a curved surface.

We shall now assume the boy wants to plane properly; he believes this is possible; and that he is capable of relating concepts. Thus he relates the concept of 'playing through the ball', which involves bodily movements such as those employed in cricket, golf and tennis, to the concept of planning. Insight is forthcoming, for 'playing through the ball' demands that the bat, club or racket be at right angles to the ball at impact and follow through in the direction which the ball is intended to follow. The young man further recognizes that 'playing through the ball' occasions certain physiological problems. These problems are caused by the relationship of limbs to joints. That is to say, each limb pivots because it has a joint about which it pivots. Therefore the locus of a point on a limb must generate a curve if one limb pivots about one joint. But if joints combine in a particular way it is possible for the locus of a limb to generate a straight line.

The crucial point of course is that our young man now understands that skills either in games or craft require mental control of physical movements. For without such control, limbs are bound to pivot in an arc rather than co-ordinate to generate a straight movement. Hence the difficulty in hitting a cricket, golf or tennis ball straight in the intended direction and the difficulty of planing a flat side on a piece of timber.

Planing can therefore be done intelligently or unintelligently, but if it is done unintelligently a flat surface cannot be produced, for physical causes of corporeal movements must necessarily result in bodily movements working in an arc of a circle. Thus planing or indeed any other craft skill is not a question of theorizing and then doing. It is as Ryle argues, a question of doing one thing and not two.

> 'Intelligent' cannot be defined in terms of 'intellectual' or 'knowing how' in terms of 'knowing that', 'thinking what I am doing' does not connote 'both thinking what to do and doing it'. When I do something intelligently, i e thinking what I am doing, I am doing one thing and not two. My performance has a special procedure or manner, not special antecedents.[9]

Hence the mind controls theorizing as it controls the performance of craft skills and both activities may be performed intelligently or unintelligently.

Consequently, D'Alembert's major premise, 'as there are rules for the operation of the mind and soul, so are there rules for the operation of the body', is false. For craft skills must be conducted intelligently if success is to be achieved and to conduct them intelligently is to do one thing and not two. Thus there can be no distinction between, 'rules for the operation of the mind and soul, and rules for the operation of the body', for if such a distinction was valid, skilled performance would not depend upon 'mental causes of corporeal movements', and we have shown that it does so depend. Therefore as D'Alembert's major premise is not true there can be no warranty for the conclusions which are deduced.

Having dealt with a craft skill and shown its cognitive element, we will now consider certain key concepts which are characteristic of craft and argue that application of these concepts cannot be made in terms of physical criteria alone. Moreover in this analysis we shall apply Hirst's criteria for formulating the characteristics of a subject:

1 the nature of the key concepts which are distinctive of the subject

2 the characteristics between the key concepts

3 the criteria according to which judgments are assessed for truth or falsity within the subject.[10]

We are concerned then with the kind of knowledge which is involved in craft for as Hirst states:

> To acquire knowledge is to become aware of experience as structured and made meaningful in some quite specific way and the varieties of human knowledge constitute the highly developed form in which man has found this possible. To acquire knowledge is to learn to see, to experience the world in a way otherwise unknown and thereby to have a mind in a fuller sense ... To have a mind basically involves

coming to have experience articulated by means of various conceptual schema. It is only because man has over a millenia objectified and progressively developed these that he has achieved the forms of human knowledge and the possibility of the development of mind as we know it is to us today.[11]

If such conceptual schema 'develop mind' and yield knowledge, what varieties of knowledge are involved in education which enable such conceptual schema to be formulated?

In educational contexts, the term 'knowledge' is frequently intended as embracing both sets of ideas: the accumulated skill and lore pertaining to technological control of the environment and those intellectual arts and experiences whose value is intrinsic to themselves. Knowledge in such contexts marks the whole content of our intellectual heritage, which education is concerned to pass on to succeeding generations.[12]

So if acquiring knowledge is 'learning to see, to experience the world in a way otherwise unknown and thereby to have a mind in a fuller sense', we must ask what distinctive concepts are there inherent in craft which enable man 'to have a mind in this fuller sense'.

The key concepts which are distinctive in craft seem to be those of design and form, these concepts being necessarily intertwined but separated for the purposes of this analysis. Both these concepts incorporate evaluative judgments; that is to say, judgments which determine the value of what has been done. Such judgments being assessed according to the criteria which are devised to test the validity of the object. But the evaluations involved in design and form are of course different in extent from the evaluation of the completed object. For the completed object represents a synthesis of the total craft process. Therefore evaluation of the completed object is concerned with the whole rather than with a part. The significance of this distinction between evaluation of part and evaluation of the whole is crucial, for a necessary requirement is that the object should achieve physical existence.

Craft then involves evaluative judgments which are assessed according to certain criteria. Moreover, whilst evaluative judgments can be made before the object achieves physical existence, some of these judgments cannot be assessed for validity until the object is completed. It follows then that craft work necessarily involves evaluation of the product, for without the product the validity of the total craft process cannot be assessed. The criteria employed to assess the validity of evaluative judgments will not however be made explicit until our analysis of design and form is complete. What then do we mean by design? There are difficulties here for as Field points out:

Design has come into fashion in the schools of art, presumably because of the Diploma in Art and Design, but does this mean that design has a synonym for art or does it mean design for industry and commerce? The latter seems more likely in which case its use is not very appropriate at present to describe what goes on in schools of general education and in Colleges of Education.[13]

We shall not regard design as being synonymous with art or as being synonymous with design in industry and commerce, although our definition could overlap those offered for these specific activities. Design in our terms is referring to 'a plan formed in the mind'[2]. A plan being taken to mean general rather than specific ideas. Design does not therefore refer to a specific activity of designing in the sense of 'Artful scheming, working for self interest, or the art of making designs or patterns'[2]. For design is conceived of here as a mental activity which connotes inventive activities of many kinds. Thus in this sense the process of design is a general notion which may be applied to particular subject boundaries within craft, which require specialist materials. It follows then according to this definition any case of design involves mental activity which results in a concept of that item being conceived in the mind.

This concept may be original in the sense that it has not 'been derived, copied or initiated by anything else'[2]. Alternatively, the concept may be original even though it is of an item well known and commonly used, for example a silver coffee pot. The sceptic could offer criticism at this point by contending that the concept of a coffee pot is in no way original, for such a concept is based on the visual experience of other coffee pots. This of course, is probably the case but it is advisable to remind ourselves of Dr Bronowski's words concerning recognition:

> We recognize the object to be the same because it is much the same, it is never exactly like it was, it is tolerably like. In the art of recognition a judgment is built in — an area of tolerance or uncertainty[14].

Design is therefore a general notion which involves cognitive activity but such cognitive activity must be expressed in visible form. A sketch thus becomes the manifestation of the idea. Even so, the design is still not physical, for it is only the paper which is physical, so we are still involved in the realm of general ideas. But the visual recognition offered by the sketch will almost certainly result in adaptations of that sketch. Such adaptations are the result of evaluative judgments. The validity of these judgments is assessed by whether they conform to criteria which have been adopted.

Also inherent in the concept of design is the selection of the appropriate materials required to transpose the idea into its finished shape. Here two further concepts are interrelated, these being materials and constructions. The concept of materials embraces mathematics, physics, biology, chemistry and metallurgy as indeed does the concept of constructions. For all materials have structures, physical states, physical properties and mechanical properties. Moreover, these physical states can be affected by 'working'. Therefore the concepts of materials and constructions are necessarily related.

But our concept is still incomplete, for the idea conceived is still in a non-physical state. Hence from sketches, adapted sketches and decisions regarding materials and constructions, must be produced what is frequently called a 'working drawing'. A working drawing is, as the term implies, a drawing which conveys what has to be done to produce the object. Such a drawing illustrates in two dimensional form the completed shape, each individual component, the exact sizes plus tolerances, and the specification of appropriate materials and constructions.

The notion of the working drawing requires further investigation for consideration of design has presented this drawing as the final formulation of the process. But working drawings as such are also the vehicle by which other persons can visualize the idea expressed by those drawings. In other words, the working drawing expresses a concept, it is not just a collection of lines embodying shapes and exact sizes, it is rather a collection of lines embodying shapes and sizes which convey to the receptive mind a three-dimensional picture of the idea in the form of an object. A working drawing enables others to see what is to be made and how it is to be made in terms of materials and constructions. It does not, of course, convey how the object is to be made in the sense of specifying how skills are actually performed.

Design is therefore a general cognitive notion which results in particular ideas. But it is obvious that not all design ideas can be transformed into physical existence. The Sydney Opera House serves as an appropriate example of the difficulties which are involved. This does not imply that ideas which do not come to fruition do not have value. Neither does it imply that ideas which pose problems of manufacture are not worthwhile, nor does it imply that the criterion of 'good' design is necessarily that manufacture is a straightforward affair. Rather it suggests that craft education is an intelligent pursuit, in which designing and making are necessarily related, for if a design is not transformed into a physical entity, it can never be evaluated as a physical entity.

However, our central point is that design is a cognitive activity, even though it does presuppose an ability to draw. But as drawing is a skill, and as a skill depends upon thinking what is being done, and as thinking about what is being done is doing one thing and not two, we do not weaken our statement.

We have considered the concept of design, we have also argued that design in craft work must be related to making, for, if it was not, no design would ever achieve physical existence. But we have not denied that design may exist as a separate entity. Our point is simply that the design of an object does not become fully meaningful unless the object is made, for final evaluation cannot be made unless that object physically exists. Therefore, 'the conflict between emphasis on creativity and emphasis on craft skills'[15] seems vacuous in that without skills, designs selected for manufacture cannot be made. Perhaps this supposed conflict is the most recent manifestation of the distinction between 'rules for the operation of the mind and rules for the operation of the body'.

However, if we contend that design is related to making, we must now consider the concept which covers this process. We shall regard this concept as that of form. In dealing with form, we shall argue that the cognitive element in a skill is not only confined to physical movements and first principles of that skill, but also concerned with the emotions. We shall accept Peter's view that:

> Any state of mind that can be called an 'emotion' such as fear, anger, jealousy or remorse, is characterized by an appraisal of an object or situation which is internally related to it. . . . How man sees a situation is basic to characterizing the state of mind as one of 'emotion' in general and as one of 'fear' or 'anger' or 'resentment' or 'jealousy' in particular. For to be so characterized a man has to see it as in general agreeable or disagreeable in a certain respect. . . . The feeling involved in 'emotion' is inseparable from the aspect under which he views the situation.[16]

We shall argue that there is a distinction between the concept of hand skills and machine skills.

Form connotes 'A shape, a mould, beauty, style, arrangement, structural unity, (and when used as a transitive verb) to give shape, to bring into being'[2]. But beauty, style, arrangement and structural unity are obviously factors dependent upon the artifact being completed; whilst mould, to give shape, to bring into being, are related to the process of construction. In turn, construction necessarily involves skills. Thus if we are talking about the feeling in emotion engendered during the construction process, we are talking about the feeling in emotion as related to skills. 'He knew not by theory but more delicately, in his eyes and fingers. The grain of the timber told secrets to them'.[17]

But as Peters points out: 'the feeling in emotion is inseparable from the aspect under which (an individual) views the situation'[16]. Hence the positive feeling in the emotion in craft skills is caused not by the plane or machine producing an uneven surface but by the plane or machine producing a true surface, with the corollary that different persons would have different feelings about this. However, as a true surface cannot be attained with blunt or uncontrolled tools, or badly set uncontrolled machines, positive or negative feelings in emotion are directly attributable to rational causes. For as our planing example demonstrated there are specific mental sequences that must be fulfilled if we are to perform skilfully.

We have argued following Peters that the feelings in emotion derived from craft skills have a rational cognitive core. Hence by establishing certain feelings in emotion have this rational cognitive core, it is not unreasonable to suggest that craft skills can encourage the pursuit of reason in relation to human emotions. For if certain feelings in emotion have a rational core, others must also have a rational cognitive core.

Therefore when we talk in terms of craft educating the emotions, we are concerned with providing children with the means by which they can view craft in a rational way. 'The feeling involved in emotion is inseparable from the aspect under which he views the situation'.[16]

Our next task is to consider the distinction between those skills which require a mind, body, tool relationship and those which require a mind, body, machine relationship. An example of the former would be planing, filing and sawing, whilst lathe operations, milling operations and soldering are examples of the latter. Both kinds of skill have in common the production of a form or shape, a mode of execution and involve feelings in emotion. Moreover both kinds of skill are directly related to the concepts of materials and constructions.

However, the chief difference between these skills is the range of the concepts involved. The planing example illustrated the relative simplicity of understanding the mind, body, and tool skill. But the concept encompassing, for example, the function and operation of a lathe is extensive. For this concept includes a welter of theory, such as the sorts of shapes which can be produced; the theory of metal cutting allied to appropriate tool and work setting, sharpening; and a thorough comprehension of the terms 'precision' and 'tolerance'. Hence,

All skilled performance is mental in the sense that knowledge and judgment are required, and all skills involve some kind of co-ordinated overt activity by hands, organs of speech or other effectors[18].

Having completed our analysis of form we must compile the evaluative criteria by which an artifact is judged. These criteria are applied throughout the process of design and form, but judgments during these stages can only be concerned with parts of the total process, for the artifact only becomes a whole when it is completed. But such criteria are exceedingly difficult to justify, for they are necessarily expressed in the form of value judgments. However, these difficulties cannot be avoided for to determine the value of anything necessarily involves a value-judgment.

We shall begin therefore, with the design process for it was here that the design was conceived in terms of an idea. But it must be explained that whilst each criterion is logically separate, all must be fulfilled if evaluation is to be complete. For evaluation in craft is an evaluation of a total process which involves the creation of an object from inception to its finished shape.

The first criterion of evaluation is 'does the finished object manifest the completion of the idea?' In other words, does the object fulfil design expectations. In craft terms, this would mean, does the coffee pot fulfil the functions of a coffee pot? Or does the pneumatic motor fulfil design specifications, that is to say, x revolutions and y horse power? The second criterion is that of construction. Will the coffee pot or pneumatic motor remain a structural unity or will it fall to pieces? Thirdly, we have the criterion of beauty or aesthetic pleasure. In other words does the coffee pot or pneumatic motor promote feelings in emotion which can be rationally explained?

We have shown in this essay, that craft involves an interrelationship of concepts and evaluative judgments. Furthermore, we have argued that the application of such concepts and evaluative judgments cannot be made in terms of physical criteria alone. Moreover, we are now in a position to conclude that craft is distinguishable from other subjects, not because of its theoretical knowledge, but rather because it contains the concept 'form'; for craft is the only activity which contains this kind of knowledge. Thus it seems ironic that the very aspect of the subject which gives it intrinsic value has been the subject of constant challenge.

References

1 D'Adembert, in *Craftsmen All*, p. 4, Dryad Press (1936)
2 *Chambers Twentieth Century Dictionary*, W & R Chambers, Glasgow (1966)
3 Bronowski J. *The Ascent of Man*, p. 211, BBC Publications (1973)
4 Ryle G. *Concept of Mind*, Hutchinson Publishing Group Ltd (1967)
5 Rickman H.P. *The Use of Philosophy*, Routledge & Kegan Paul Ltd (1973)
6 Ryle G. *op. cit.* p. 19
7 Ryle G. *op. cit.* p. 22
8 Magee J.B. *Philosophical Analysis in Education*, p. 6, Harper & Row Ltd (1972)
9 Ryle G. *op. cit.* p. 32
10 Gribble J. *Introduction to Philosophy of Education*, p. 49, Allyn & Bacon, Boston (1969)
11 Archambault R.D. Ed. *Philosophical Analysis and Education* pp. 124-5, Routledge & Kegan Paul Ltd (1970)
12 Scheffler I. *Conditions of Knowledge: An Introduction to Epistemology and Education*, p. 2, Scott Foresman & Co, Illinois (1965)
13 Field D. *Change in Art Education*, p. 3, Routledge and Kegan Paul Ltd (1970)
14 Bronowski J. *op. cit.* p. 365
15 Eggleston J. *Studies in Design Education and Craft,* Vol. 5, No. 2, p. 3 University of Keele (Spring 1973)
16 Peters R.S. *Ethics and Education,* p. 110, George Allen and Unwin (1971)
17 Sturt G. *The Wheelwright's Shop,* pp. 54-55, Cambridge University Press (1963)
18 Welford A.T., D. Legge Ed., *In Skills,* p. 22, Penguin Books Ltd (1970)

6
Technical graphics in schools

A.P.P. DURANT

Percy Durant was formerly Head of the Department of Design at Hilsea Modern School, Portsmouth. He is Chairman/Consortium Secretary of the Design Committee for the Southern Region Examinations Board, has been a Chief Examiner in technical drawing, and has lectured in graphics at ICED summer schools. This paper has been sponsored by Hartley Reece and Co.

Abstract   This paper describes the contribution technical graphics can make to design education. It considers basic aims, examination requirements, techniques and equipment.

Behind the title Technical Graphics lies a quiet revolution that is sweeping through the nation's schools. Is this just another education gimmick? Another brief spin-off from ROSLA? Another short lived hare-brained scheme? I do not think so and here I hope to make a case that will convince the sceptics.

The use of the title Technical Graphics highlights a considerable change in educational philosophy, a change that is continuing with increasing momentum. What the long term effect will be on technical drawing as a school subject is difficult to assess at this time, but it can be stated with truth that in many schools it is already resulting in considerable change, a change that many teachers are convinced is for the better.

Let me first attempt briefly to define the terms Technical Drawing and Technical Graphics used in the context of classroom teaching.

Traditionally Technical Drawing has included plain and solid geometry, orthogonal projection and common pictorial projections. The work has been executed in pencil on white paper. The drawings have been largely workshop based and secondary to the main workshop processes.

The introduction of Technical Drawing as an 'O' level subject marked a significant change in attitude to the subject. It became a subject in its own right, too much so in some cases where it became remote from its basic relationship with workshops. Certainly it can be stated that considerable significant changes in drafting standards can be attributed to the influence of 'O' level teaching, the improvement continuing and spreading to the less able student through the opportunities offered by the CSE examination.

Technical Graphics, in the context of secondary education is very different. True it includes Technical Drawing, but much more besides. It serves a large area of the school curriculum. Its scope takes in all the vast area between workshop and art studio. It is important to subjects such as Design and Technical Illustration, to name but two that were not even on the timetable a few years ago.

Among the sub-headings can be grouped, in addition to Technical Drawing as traditionally taught, measured perspective, advertising design, logos, book illustration, drawings of schematic lay-outs, mathematical diagrams, charts, architectural and marine drawing and in fact any drawing that has technical requirements. The scope is clearly vast and obviously significant to any school, whether urban or town based.

The value of the subject lies in this versatility. Given a sound basic course in which the required techniques are taught, the subject can be treated as being entirely open-ended.

Students are excited by Technical Graphics from their very first lesson. It matters not whether they have studied Technical Drawing before, this is something new, something different. A whole new world of drawing is revealed.

Two factors that stand out as having influence above all others are the use of the drafting pen and the use of colour, and of these the medium with the greater initial impact is the pen.

Practically any third or fourth year student can, if properly taught and if provided with a good pen produce a simple and smudge-free drawing after the first one or two efforts. The effect is magical! Here, instead of the previous pencil line of varying widths and densities is a crisp, authoritative drawing with black ink line on white paper, just like the textbook. The 'looks like it's printed, sir' remark may bring a smile to the face of the teacher, but it is a very understandable, a very human reaction. Add to this the use of a printing stencil giving splendid looking letters instead of poorly formed pencil work, and the effect is magical.

The boost to morale is immediate, and the poorer the past performance of the student, the greater is the psychological lift. Messy handed lads find that they can erase most, if not all of the grubbiness from their drawings that in the past has been so difficult and discouraging.

One predictable effect of using the drafting pen is the obvious feeling of superiority that any class experiences over others whose work is confined to pencil. Used in the fourth and fifth years of secondary education, the ink line, producing as it does a 'professional' finish, accords well with the desires of the upper school student to do things that are different, grown-up, mature.

Colour too can have a dramatic effect on young people's work, whether it is applied in order to enhance the appearance of the drawing or to serve a specific structural purpose. The use of colour fulfils a deep, even primitive need in man. If used properly in the classroom this can lead to a high degree of motivation in the student.

Probably the biggest single influence affecting the present swing from traditional Technical Drawing to Technical Graphics is the emergence of Design as an integrated subject area in schools. The multimedia approach to craft education is causing the breaking down of barriers between woodwork and metalwork and the like. More and often 'newer' subjects are being added to the curriculum in order to cater for the needs of the modern student. Central to the whole of the Design Studies area is the need for drawing as a means of communication, drawing broadly based and able to cater equally for the workshop based craft and one that is art based, and for anything in between.

It will be obvious that Technical Graphics needs to be taught as a broadly based subject. The teacher must be familiar with the special needs of colleagues covering a wide range of subject areas. He must be aware of the interdependence of these subject areas and must bring this home to the student. Above all, he must teach his subject in such a way that Technical Graphics is seen to perform a unifying role in the teaching of Design.

Since so much of Design work is executed in three dimensions, the graphics will need to have much time spent on pictorial projections, perspective drawings and freehand sketches. To these basic drawings must be added the representation of texture and colour. These last two factors, texture and colour, are very important. The use of the correct techniques can add the equivalent of an extra dimension to many drawings. Not less important is the effect produced on the student by these two factors, particularly colour. The extra interest on the part of the student generated by the production of 'live' drawing is reflected in more interest, more motivation and then, by a sort of compound interest, a higher standard of performance that can be truly impressive.

A few words need to be said about the Technical Graphics syllabus and its relationship with others in the Design group. There will obviously be areas of overlap with the Art syllabus since colour is involved. In the craft areas graphics will be used during the normal craft lessons. The craft teacher will, after the course has been running for a time, assume knowledge of graphics on the part of the student and will apply that knowledge and these particular skills to the illustration of class and individual projects. Closely defined syllabi and close and continuing dialogue between all Design staff will be imperative. Any slackening of attention to this aspect of integration would not only result in a waste of time but would tend to lead to a feeling of frustration on the part of the student.

In planning the Technical Graphics syllabus some rough generalizations may be made, whether the work is tied to Design or has a more specialized application to Technical Illustration or Architectural Drawing, Advertising or some other field.

To get the course off to a flying start the drafting pens should be introduced. The subject of the drawing is not important so long as it is easy and requires little learning of new facts. The mastery of the pen is the object of the exercise and all other difficulties should be smoothed away. The use of the ink compass is best left out of the first few drawings as it is one more complication that is best avoided. Given this concentration of effort on plain ink drafting, the teacher can expect a small number of students to produce a smudge-free drawing the first time and perfect drawings from practically all students after the first three drawings, given a normal cross section of intelligence with Fourth Year students.

These first drawings can have a single subject drawn in various projections if the students are already familiar with the principles from their studies in conventional Technical Drawing lessons. If the students have no previous experience, then simple straight line patterns copied from a text book would be suitable. From the first the students should be made aware of the need for good spacing of the drawing on paper and of the need for clear and tastefully arranged printing.

Quite early in the course it is advisable to introduce single and two point unmeasured perspective as being a medium of great value to a wide area of curriculum studies. Early practice with colour can be introduced through the use of crayon pencils, for although the colours produced are not very exciting, the pencils are cheap and easy to

find a part-tin of the stuff at home that is not wanted and are happy to put it to a good use. Trial on scrap paper is important, of course, and often the stuff needs straining through a silk stocking, but it is really useful for so many jobs.

The possession of an air brush is a boon. The great thing about its use, from the pupils' point of view, is the absence of brush-marks in the art work. Large expanses of paper can receive a solid colour or can exploit spatter techniques and similar effects. Masking techniques can also prove useful, enabling a controlled build up to take place with little risk to the final effect. Also, of course, the air brush can produce effects unique to the process.

It would be nice to round off this paper with a neat summing-up, making a tidy package of the whole thing. I really cannot. The subject of Technical Graphics is too vast. There is far more of the subject left out of this paper than is written in. The techniques are so varied, ranging from the very simple to the very complex, the needs of the schools so diverse that neat schemes of work cannot be prescribed. One can only advise one's colleagues to give Technical Graphics a trial in their own school settings and to assess the results.

What is so very rewarding is the manner in which students of Technical Graphics can continue the education of their teachers! Once they appreciate the possibilities for experiment and discovery inherent in the study, the pupils will constantly be finding new ways of getting effects, new methods of presentation and new end products and that cannot be anything but good.

7
Examining design and craft
P. E. DUTTON

Peter E. Dutton is the Liaison Officer of the Sheffield Region Centre for Science and Technology based on Sheffield Polytechnic. Since the formation of the Centre in 1970, he has been involved with craft teachers on several projects including a probe into the use of projects, a development course on local communications, some work on industrial archaeology and the major scheme reported here on examining design and craft. He is currently working on an idea of how to increase technological literacy through craft work.

Abstract This paper traces the background and describes the approach to the establishment of an examination in design and craft. It covers aims and objectives and gives details of both schemes of work and assessment procedures.

Introduction
Late in 1972, a working party was established by the Associated Examining Board and the West Yorkshire and Lindsey Regional Examining Board (TWYLREB) to prepare a feasibility study for a single examination at sixteen + in the field of design and craft. This was part of the scheme run by Schools Council to look at the problems faced by all subjects if an examination was taken at sixteen + years by all school pupils within the 40th to 100th percentiles. The Chairman of the working party was Mr N.B. Fortune, General Adviser (Design and Craft) with the Sheffield LEA, and membership included eight teachers specializing in different aspects of craft work, three advisers, one each from colleges of education and further education and representatives of the two Boards and Schools Council.

A draft scheme was circulated to all TWYLREB schools in Autumn 1973 and discussed at three meetings with craft teachers. Considerable modifications were made to the detail of the scheme which was published in its final form early in 1974. Eleven schools took part in the formal feasibility study in Summer 1975, entering 168 candidates for the examination. At the moment of writing (July 1975), the results of this examination are not known and the formal Report to Schools Council on the feasibility study has to be submitted by December 1975. Both will be discussed at the Conference in April 1976. It will be noted that there is no syllabus in the accepted sense but a statement of aims and objectives. These become the criteria for the setting and marking of questions.

Educational philosophy on which the examination is based

Scope of the examination

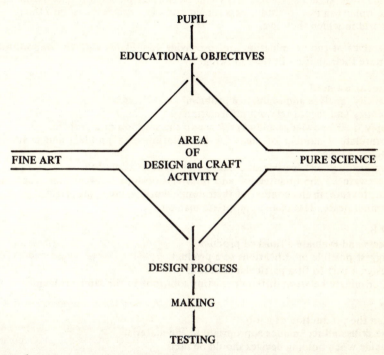

Diagram 1

Diagram 1 illustrates the indistinct boundaries that exist between Design and Craft activity, and Fine Art and Pure Science. For the benefit of candidates and teachers it should be stated at the outset that there is no prescribed syllabus for the examination. Any design problem which has a tangible solution may be described, for purposes of this examination, as falling within the area of Design and Craft activity. It must, however, be possible to evaluate any solution to the problem in accordance with the following criteria:

1 (a) are the chosen materials appropriate?
   (b) is the structure appropriate to the materials used?
   (c) have appropriate techniques been used?

2 does it solve the design problem and have the materials, structure and techniques been used in sympathy with, and consideration for, the appearance of the final product in its context?

Aims and objectives of the examination
The aims are as follows:
to foster a degree of understanding and expertise in those areas of creative thinking which can be expressed and developed through planning and working with materials
to provide situations which encourage pupils to use their practical and intellectual skills in design experiences, operating through a process of analysis, synthesis and realization in a variety of materials
to promote the development of initiative, ingenuity, resourcefulness, self-involvement, co-operation, social responsibility and the ability to communicate
to encourage students to relate the course to their personal interests and thereby create opportunities to study, experiment and carry out research into the nature of the world in which they live.

The objectives of the examination are to provide candidates with the opportunity to demonstrate their abilities in the following:
GROUP A:
to recognize a need
to identify, analyse and evaluate a problem
to identify and record relevant information
to apply their knowledge and experience to the solution of a problem
to formulate a number of ideas for the solution of a problem and examine the feasibility of each
to develop the most feasible of a number of ideas to a solution
to be aware of the qualities of and interrelationships between line, form, space, colour, texture, in the context of their design work where appropriate
to communicate ideas in an appropriate manner

GROUP B:
to assess and evaluate a finished product
to suggest possible modifications to a product
to design a part to fit a particular situation
to discriminate between different existing solutions to the same problem

GROUP C:
to plan the production of a job
to use skills and techniques appropriate to the material
to decide when holding devices should be used
to use jigs, patterns, formers or moulds to assist operations
to decide the kind of finish and standard of accuracy necessary for a particular piece of work
to be critical of personal standards of work
to use equipment and materials with care and safety, and be aware of the social responsibilities involved
to anticipate dangers and take appropriate action.

The form of the examination
There will be three components to the examination, namely:
(a) Course Work
(b) Paper 1 — Design and Realization of Design
(c) Paper 2 — Design and Communication

Course Work will be assessed. Papers 1 and 2 will be externally set and externally marked. In the mark for the examination as a whole, equal weighting will be given to Course Work and the External Examination. In order to qualify for the award of a certificate candidates must present evidence of work in more than one material and must also attempt all three components of the examination.

(a) Course work

For the purposes of the examination the following aspects of Course Work will be assessed separately.

1 The whole of the work the candidate has done for this examination during a period of five terms in the two years immediately prior to the examination (or, in the case of candidates from Colleges of Further Education or in post-fifth year courses, the two terms immediately prior to the examination) other than work done specifically for (2).

2 A significant piece of Course Work of the candidate's own choice which has been selected to demonstrate his understanding of the design process from the problem to the finished product. This must be supported by a design folio.

Group projects will be acceptable as Course Work provided that

1 the contribution made by each candidate can be clearly identified

2 this does not constitute the only Course Work submitted by any candidate.

Course Work, except for the 'making process', will be assessed internally in accordance with the draft guide lines provided below, and moderated by Inter-school assessment. Agreement Trials will be arranged in this connection. Operational Agreement Trials, for the appointment of Inter-school Assessors, will also be arranged.

(b) Examination Paper 1 – Design and Realization of Design

1 The question paper for this examination will be issued to schools by 1st February in the year when the examination is due to be held. It will contain a number of questions from which each candidate will select one. The candidate will be required to submit the design folio and final realization of the solution to the chosen problem by 30th April.

2 The allocation of time for the solution of the design problem between 1st February and 30th April will be left to the discretion of the teacher, with the stipulation that not more than six hours, spread over two or more sessions, should be spent on the realization. The realization itself need not be completed. Any patterns, moulds or jigs required for the realization must be submitted with the realization for assessment, but the time taken in making them does not count against the six hours.

3 The design folio presented with the realization must include:

(a) an analysis of the design problem

(b) the postulation of possible solutions, feasibility of ideas being ignored at this stage

(c) the selection, development and feasibility of the preferred idea

(d) the communication and presentation of the chosen solution

(e) the candidate's justification for this solution

(f) the candidate's written appraisal of the solution after the realization has been done, and any further modifications that he or she wishes to suggest.

4 When the candidate has completed his/her design and prior to starting the realization, he or she may, if necessary, modify the solution in consultation with the teacher, ascertaining that it will be feasible and can be made up in the material chosen. Equally, the candidate may make any modification while carrying out the realization. The reason for these modifications must be clearly stated in the candidate's appraisal of the finished product. All modifications made by either the class teacher or the candidate must be clearly recorded.

43

(c) Examination Paper 2 – Design and Communication

1 This paper will be of one and a half hours duration plus fifteen minutes reading time.
2 The paper will be divided into Section 1 and Section 2. Section 1 will consist of questions based primarily, but not entirely, on the objectives set out in Group B above. Section 2 will consist of questions based primarily, but not entirely, on the objectives set out in Group C above.
3 Candidates will be required to answer two questions, one from each section.
4 Forty per cent of the total marks for the paper will be allocated to Section 1 and sixty per cent to Section 2.

Draft guide lines for the assessment of Course Work

The Grading System
Eight grades are available for the assessment of Course Work. They are set out in diagram 2 with their GCE and CSE equivalents. Not every school will need to use the whole of the grading scale.

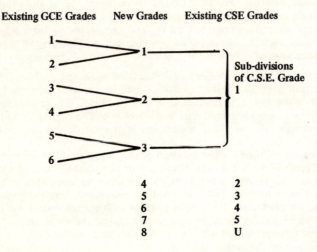

Diagram 2

The assessment of Course Work
There are three areas to be assessed, namely: the design folio, the making process, the finished product. It is convenient, in the first place, to consider the second of these areas, because Inter-school assessment is not involved.

The making process
In determining the grade for the making process, equal weighting should be attached to the operations mentioned under (i), (ii) and (iii) in table 1. Only the teacher can assess these operations because the assessment must be made while the work is in progress. The teacher's grade will be accepted without further validation.

Table 1

Operation	Criteria for Assessment
(i) Personal involvement	Evidence of personal involvement as outlined in the aims of the examination
(ii) Planning the stages of production	In relation to the complexity of the job and the amount of help given by the teacher
(iii) Use of skills	Ability to use skills already acquired Ability to acquire and use new skills appropriate to the job

The design folio
In the assessment of the design folio, equal importance should be attached to (ii), (iii) and (iv) in table 2; (i) is of less significance and should not be allowed to influence the assessment otherwise obtained, by more than one grade in either direction.

Table 2

Operation	Criteria for Assessment
(i) Identification of need	Degree of pupil initiative
(ii) Analysis of problem	Identification of problem Analysis of relevant factors Evidence of investigation
Postulation of possible solutions (Feasibility of ideas to be ignored at this stage)	Variety of ideas Clarity of communication
(iii) Selection, development and feasibility of preferred idea	Relevance to brief Study of materials, constructions, components and costs Evidence of experiment and the use of models or 'mock-ups' where appropriate
(iv) Communication and presentation of solution	Comprehensiveness Clarity

The finished product
In the assessment of the finished product, attention should, in the main, be focused on workmanship, i.e. on (i) in table 3. The operations included under (ii) should not be allowed to affect the assessment by more than one grade either way.

Table 3

Operation	Criteria for Assessment
(i) Workmanship	Workmanship as demonstrated by the finished product (The design and its success as a solution to the problem to be ignored)
(ii) Aspects of design which can only be evaluated in the finished product	Quality of inter-relationships between line, form, space, colour and texture in relation to the parts of the product itself and of the product in its environment

Conclusion

Without prejudice to the Report to Schools Council of this feasibility study, the author states that in his opinion this type of examination is an undoubted success. Several aspects will have to be changed in the light of experience, but the overall philosophy has been shown to be educationally viable. It is possible for a wide range of young people to benefit from experiences with different materials using the fundamental design approach to their craft work and for that benefit to be assessed realistically by an examination of the form described. Everybody associated with the working party and the examination has also benefitted personally — it has been a most enjoyable and worthwhile exercise.

8
Are we teaching bad design?

D. GRADY

Derrick Grady is Warden of the Education Centre, Kingston upon Hull. He is past president of the Institute of Craft Education, has been Head of Technical Studies at a large comprehensive school following wide experience as a practising craftsman and teacher.

Abstract   This paper discusses the nature of design and the components of design education in terms of school methodology. It covers both intrinsic and developmental considerations and suggests a strategy for implementation.

As a young student I remember spending much time discussing with both colleagues and tutors the distinction between 'good' and 'bad' design. This was in the immediate post war period when the 'Britain Can Make It' Exhibition and Festival of Britain again illuminated design as a fundamental activity for an industrialized nation. Notions generated in the Bauhaus and at Ulm were accepted and rapidly became teaching bases mainly because of availability and apparent relevance. Industrial design grew into a flourishing subject at many art colleges. The rule of form, function and fitness for purpose was almost absolute. Later developments of analytical approaches, largely based on research for computer programming, emerged with systematic methodology encouraging belief that problem solving was indeed design. Curiously, it was among students that an instinctive, almost subconscious, recognition of a missing element grew. It was and remains mysterious, difficult to define but necessary for production of design quality. J.R. Tolkien in his essay 'On Fairy Stories' takes us to the heart of the matter.

We are therefore confronted with the problem encountered by archaeologists: the debate between independent evolution (or rather invention) of the similar; inheritance from a common ancestry; and diffusion at various times from one or more centres. All three have evidently played their part in producing the intricate web of (design?)

(It is indeed easier to unravel a single thread than to trace the history of any picture defined by many threads. For with the picture in the tapestry a new element has come in: the picture is greater than, and not explained by, the sum of the component threads. Therein lies the inherent weakness of the analytic [or scientific] method: it finds out much about things that occur, but little or nothing about their effects.)

Of these three, invention is the most important and fundamental, and so (not surprisingly) also the most mysterious. To an inventor the other two must in the end lead back. Diffusion (borrowing in space) of an artifact only refers the problem of origin elsewhere. At the centre of the supposed diffusion there is a place where once an inventor lived. Similarly with inheritance, (borrowing in time): in this way we arrive at last only at an ancestral inventor.

We must recognize, therefore, that form, function, fitness for purpose and problem solving are all involved in design activity and contribute towards design quality but require the spark of invention, creativity, even genius for its emergence.

Recognizing that definition of values is almost impossible, since these relate mainly to social development and are adapted, modified or altered as circumstances vary, flexible attitudes are more constructive. Also, it is not the purpose of this essay to become entangled in controversy over meanings. Yet, there exists a discernable quality about many ideas and products which render them impervious to modes of fashion. Equally, others are objectionable and, however durable, are recognizably so even when cloaked with the respectability of old age. The former possess an aptness which gives a sesne of rightness in any environment and for the latter, the opposite applies. It is on this distinction concepts of 'good' and 'bad' in design largely rest, and it forms the foundation for my thesis. It might be desirable to analyse why one article exhibits this quality and another does not, with questions of balance between form, function and so on assessed. This is of little relevance since my argument is not about existence of the phenomenon, but whether it can be attained by pupils using design methodology employed at present in secondary schools.

Examination syllabuses, over-riding and inescapable curriculum influences, suggest methods of work in good faith as teacher guidance. Too often these harden into rigid codes of practice leaving little room for innovation. The London University GCE Design and Technology syllabus is a classic example. Its detailed syllabus for design quotes: 'A candidate's solution to design problems could well be offered under the following headings: (a) statement, (b) analysis, (c) synthesis, (d) realization. It is hoped that wherever possible all the course work will be the result of this comprehensive and complete process'. The A level syllabus is extended to include a personal evaluation and consideration of environmental factors. Heavily influenced by Bloom's *Taxonomy of Educational Objectives,* currently in vogue at the time of the examination's inception, this format has now become almost a compulsory requirement. Yet, Jones[1] sets out no less than thirty-five procedures offering ample opportunity for the analytical assessment beloved and considered essential by examiners. The principle involved here is sharply illustrated by David Pye[2] in his exposition on the development of a lever. It is simply that concentrated and directed mental activity will always produce some measurable results in terms of problem solving directly related to (a) time elapsed, and (b) depth of involvement. This ought to have important consequences for examinations based on structures exampled above.

Of course, examinations present difficulties for design education from many viewpoints. Much of the work is virtually unexaminable by conventional means. Set-piece design problems used as examination questions tend to produce stereotype responses. This is particularly true for secondary schools where group teaching inevitably forms the majority of teacher-pupil contact up to O level. Also, tightly specified examiner expectations, exemplified by syllabus instructions instanced earlier, reinforced by result experience, easily translate teacher guidance and pupil activity into an exercise in satisfying requirements. Thus, by a more involved route, undesirable effects of past examinations reappear. Opportunity for original response is limited and the search for quality stunted.

Therefore, while it is clear that some present methodology can ensure output this may have little effect on quality. So, those who attempt to lead their pupils towards this elusive element in design work face not only inherent difficulties but also reward hurdles. Consequently, some facets of the system governing work in schools ensure only moderate response to design stimuli in which quality of output becomes submerged by need to satisfy problem solving requirements. It follows, without question, that much done will comprise 'bad' design. It may be argued with questionable justification that claimed educational effects are operative whether output is 'good' or 'bad' and these outweigh other considerations in a mass-education context. In my opinion this is a retreat from the traditional school position as promoter of excellence and constitutes an intolerable abdication of standards.

Having arrived at what may be seen my many as an extreme view, the temptation is strong to leave the matter in this unequivocal position. However, some explanation is owed if only to clarify my reasoning. The strictures on design activity in secondary schools are immense. Time allocation, period regulation, timetable setting, class group numbers, teacher education, pupil motivation, accommodation, material availability, cost limitation, these and other factors militate against real impact on the problem of design teaching. The fact that teachers have overcome many difficulties and taken their pupils into realms even of problem-solving verges on the miraculous. But, this ought not to be equated with being more than a starting point for design education. I am sure our colleagues in higher education, aware of the situation and recognizing its value as early work rightly dismiss any wilder claims. The plain fact is that school work up to O level by its very nature can do no more than identify promising pupils. That many such do not reveal their talents has been a continuing tragedy and forms the basis of numerous attempted reforms. My major concern therefore focuses on identification presently achieved being mostly of problem-solvers who are not necessarily designers.

Many teachers would say that it is only in sixth form work that restrictions disappear and some concentration on quality becomes possible. No doubt many factors are concerned and student maturity is not least, but a drive towards improved standards in early work is both necessary and attainable. Any study in this article of ingredients necessary for increased attention to quality of output must perforce be sketchy. The case is restricted by lack of space rather than abundance of possible opportunities. By far the most effective means of promoting rapid improvement lies in a thorough review of public examination methods and syllabuses. Instances quoted only need generally tightening coupled with recognition of alternative patterns of work to create an eminently satisfying course conclusion and useful assessment. Equally important is increased teacher-pupil contact time. (Since this is true for every element of the curriculum, it is obvious that apportionment is necessary. This may not always be equitable and the struggle for equality here must continue.) Careful management of allocated time and promotion of improvement related activities not dependent on teacher involvement give scope for wider initiative. Every school and teacher will produce proposals and schemes dictated by circumstances and their priorities. As examples I give below details of simple problems and ways in which I approached their containment if not solution.

An almost universal need in design work is reasonable drawing ability. Most of my pupils received little formal instruction owing to timetable restrictions. Any way in which drawing practice could be achieved was at least worthy of consideration. By listening to authorities and examining my own experience it became clear that some form of life drawing could help. Certainly, a relatively concentrated period of drawing from a model was an important influence on my own skill. As a means of encouraging observation and discipline it is unequalled if slightly out-moded. Whole figure drawing is not necessary, as Leonardo de Vinci instanced with his well-known drawings of hands, and everyone is equipped with readily available models. Youngsters who would claim no great drawing ability often produce lively, interesting and competent drawings in the form of doodles. If these two activities are brought together, useful drawing practice takes place in moments of boredom. Patternwork, sketched perspective and proportion can also be included and a valuable time addition gained.

A second problem aspect for me is the need to promote persistence of effort. Too often pupils are reluctant to explore their first ideas further. Content in accepting initial responses they become impatient as unrealities are identified. Accustomed to instant apparent perfection, a necessary concomitant of mass produced goods, this expectation influences their attitude to designing. Also, school time structures inhibit lengthy consideration of ideas. Some external influence was needed which would direct attention to the need for realistic solutions. Assessment by people outside school seemed to be a possible solution. But, for ease of operation communication must be simple, direct and involve the pupils in a central role. Consumer research by each pupil on his or her own customers, (ie their families), easily produced the best results. An added dimension was given to even the smallest design project. Other relevant design criteria appeared, the most significant of these being consumer demand usually expressed in terms of solution preference. This means initial submission of alternative schemes, thus stimulating consideration of differing design solutions. By adopting this ploy pupils became self-motivated towards trying different ideas, an invaluable element of reality was gained and, later, some sources for additional finance appeared as special projects were originated by customers.

Another important element in helping pupils to attain quality improvement is an expansion of their cultural background. Standards of design and workmanship were enforced in the past by a powerful elite who deliberately developed advanced tastes (e.g. The Grand Tour). Their reaction to poor work or designs was instinctive and impoverishing for the craftsman trader. Pressure to produce high quality work was an enforced motivation. From such crude exploitation came many masterpieces. Now, these degrading influences no longer apply and quality has become a matter of professional pride, competence and integrity controlled only by economic factors and customer acceptance. A future trend likely to arise from consumer guidance services is a new form of accountability. Preparation for working in a world where every output is scrutinized may well consist of simulated exercises in craftsman-customer relations. Role-playing has important educational impact and contributes to pupil motivation. If this can be given the bonus of reality so much the better. (Many ventures undertaken during the Design and Craft project at the University of Keele clearly come into this category, ie the Factory Day and School based production units). While such activities and their preparation may inherently contain elements of cultural enrichment, deliberate attempts to foster individual development must become established curriculum items. The traditional method of exposing cultural influences to pupils by educational visits and exchanges is equally important for sensory and language development. This is particularly true of prolonged visits at locations with international significance. Agencies concerned in this field should be alerted to their responsibilities since many concentrate wholly on language aspects.

Finally, I come to a matter of some personal concern. Other forms of expression, writing, painting, music, sculpture and so on, all become subject to critical assessment at some stage, a major component of which is evaluation of practitioner interpretation. This rarely occurs with respect to articles of craftwork. Even pots escape. The fact that every hand-wrought piece is an interpretation of an idea never seems to register. (Articles made either partially or wholly by machine process do not possess this quality, because formers, templates and jigs reduce interpretive opportunity). It is exceptional to encounter craftsmen who include analysis of this factor when looking at work. This is doubtless owing to lack of opportunity for comparison between original concept media, (sketches, mock ups, and so on), and finished work. By far the most concentrated attention is given to items of great age. These are either of historical and archaeological importance or of antique value. Samples are barely examined for aspects of craftsmanship and never assessed as examples of interpretation. Indeed, and this can hardly be understood, they are venerated merely as a result of survival. Yet many examples of pattern books exist, particularly in the field of antiques, and comparison is possible. There can be little wonder at misappropriation of public interest particularly when retention of financial value is an important issue. Of increasing importance are similar attitudes emerging with regard to new work. Scarcity of skilled craftsmen in many fields is producing an inordinate respect for hand-wrought goods. This has not attracted much attention from consumer protection agencies, and exploitation is unchecked. Informed critical assessment is an essential ingredient of estimation of design quality, and degree of interpretive success is a major element in this process. Design Education, therefore, ought to include opportunity for variety of interpretation with recognition equal to that accorded innovation.

I hope that enough has been included in the brief confines of this article to indicate wider dimensions for design education in secondary schools. Concentration on narrow approaches merely because they can be readily absorbed into a curriculum context is an ever-present hazard. In this connection, interaction between teachers from differing subject disciplines is a vital component of progress. Therefore, development of integrated schemes of work with all their attendant difficulties is a necessary function and not a fashionable movement. It should also be realized that this process is lengthy, requires abundant support and is most effective when implemented by teachers within the direct teaching situation concerned. Constant and rigorous examination of every stage is necessary to ensure that spurious side-effects, as quoted above regarding school examinations, do not assume dominance. Since this essay is an attempt to provide an element of such scrutiny, it is hoped those concerned will accept these opinions at least as a practical contribution, even if mine is a lone voice.

References
1 Jones J. Christopher *Design Methods,* Wiley-Interscience (1970)
2 Pye D. *The Nature of Design,* Chap. 4. Studio Vista (1964)

9
The three cultures

G.B. HARRISON

G.B. Harrison is Director of the National Centre for School Technology. He is late Head of the Department of Creative Design at Loughborough College of Education and was Director of Schools Council Project Technology.

Abstract   This paper points to the total interdependence of art, craft and technology. It comments on the apparent 'creative snobbery' of artists, craftsmen and engineers and it argues for mutual acceptance of educational responsibilities across these three fields and the avoidance of a 'three culture' syndrome.

Introduction

It has become more and more apparent in recent years that the 'two cultures' social syndrome has its counterpart in the craft fields in the schools. Perhaps it is not a matter of *two* cultures so much as a *three*-sided cultural blockage in the educational system.

Does the artist really accept that the craftsman is capable of original and creative productive activity? Does the craftsman believe that the artist's 'airy-fairy' ideals have practical applications and that the artist can ever learn to use tools properly and with sensitivity? Do either the artist or the craftsman, both of whom, of course, have souls, live by creative inspiration and are sensitive to their own environment, do they believe that the engineer is anything other than a mechanical oaf, devoid of sensitivity, visual perception, and appreciation of the pure craft skills. I hesitate to put the other side and ask if the engineer believes that either the artist or the craftsman have anything of practical value to offer the world!

The problem is similar to that which has dogged the professional engineering and scientific institutions of the country for over a hundred years. Did it all start with the controversy over who invented the miners' safety lamp? Was it Sir Humphrey Davy, of the Royal Society, or was it George Stephenson, the uneducated colliery engineman from Wylam? Which have we been led to believe through our own school education?

A similar problem shows itself in the dilemma faced by science teachers who wonder whether they should accept responsibilities for teaching about the applications and implications, in addition to the fundamentals, of their subjects. C.P. Snow's theme of the two cultures, which suggests that ours is a nation made up of scientifically illiterate arts men and artistically ignorant and insensitive scientists, is only a hint of the divisions which really exist, once the various form of intellectual snobbery are recognized.

Looking on the brighter side, the Institute of Craft Education by virtue of the fact that it is holding this symposium, demonstrates its policy of non-alignment or, at least, non-isolationism and open-mindedness. It is easy to demonstrate that art, craft and technology cannot in fact exist on their own in isolation. What forms of art are there that are not dependent upon craftsmanship and technology? Even the cave artists required their dyes to be extracted from plants and soils. The water-colour artist requires his paints, paper and brushes, all of which are technological even in their most primitive forms. What kind of craftsmanship is there which is not dependent on technology? If the fine cutting edge is one of the essential elements of craftsmanship, then there lies a technological need.

The theme of this paper is to draw attention to the essential unity of art, craft and technology, their *total* interdependence and, at least as far as education is concerned, the beneficial broadening effect each has on the others. I hope that the artists and craftsmen of the Institute will accept these comments from a mere

51

engineer who gets more pleasure out of creating with his hands than he did as an engineer on the drawing board with his slide-rule, log tables and data sheets.

A range of creative activities
All teachers will accept that one of their principal responsibilities is to help their pupils to become as creative and as individual as possible. We do not, I hope, feel that all we are expected to do is to fill up our charges with knowledge and skill in order that they may be best suited to adapt to society and accept its pressures with passivity. It is self evident that craft teachers, in particular, recognize and value this creative opportunity and responsibility. How, though, do we specify or select the possible fields in which we might help children to become more creative and individual? Do we define them first and foremost in terms of our *own* personal interests and disciplines? Should I, a woodwork master, concentrate only on helping children to become creative users of wood? Or does he, a technical draftsman, believe that technical drawing is the only line worthy of study by his pupils. Are we able, in other words, to accept, genuinely, that pupils may be interested in other activities than those of our own specialism and that we might have a part to play in encouraging pupils to locate fields of creative interest and aptitude quite different from our own?

Let us avoid the arrogance implied in the presentation of narrow opportunities. Rather, let us accept that we all have a common aim, which is to help children to discover the delight of making things, both for themselves and for others, which actually perform to a specified function and meet a well defined and recognized need. On the one hand, we must feel sorry for those who never experience this delight, and on the other hand we must recognize that this delight, pride and satisfaction can appear and be equally real for the potter, the cabinet maker, the sculptor, the toy maker, the boat builder, the radio 'ham', the silversmith, and many others.

It is here that the first real plug for technology comes because it suggests that there may be new and quite different fields in which pupils may be creative. Hi-fi, telecommunications, automatic control devices, aircraft, ships, telescopes and other optical instruments are fields which might appear to be more technological than some but which switch on *some* children to real creative efforts. However they do not often appear in traditional wood or metal working departments despite the fact that when it comes to the point a very great deal of the work is in those traditional materials.

Technology — an educational responsibility and opportunity
As teachers, we must accept the responsibility to be continuously looking outside our work and professional thinking. What is it that society, of which we are, after all, the hired servants, really wants from us teachers? Our children, growing up in a social system which is dependent, in an increasingly obvious way, on technology for its resources, its energy, its transport and communication, and indeed its whole economic structure, must become competent to make   decisions   which have technological considerations. The need for such decisions lies in the home, at work, in the community, everywhere. Do we help our children become better able to make such decisions by showing them how to identify specific problems, recognize genuine constraints, synthesize possible solutions and work out which is the 'best' when so many conflicting constraints have to be balanced one against the other?

Moreover, should we feel that such decisions can only be made in the abstract, such as 'do I decide to have double glazing fitted to my windows?', or 'should I switch off the immersion heater at nights?'. Or do we feel that our pupils may become even more personally involved in the technological process itself as a result of some of these decisions? Any do-it-yourself householder (and who isn't one?) is inevitably engaging, personally, in the technological process. The installation of shelving, alterations to electrical wiring, erection of a garden shed, car or motorcycle repairs and maintenance, these are simple everyday samples of engagement in technology. But our children are also the workforce, at all levels, of the future. They will be our farmers, road-makers, water-supply men, electrical technicians and engineers, gas fitters, builders, decorators, railwaymen, bus drivers, hospital maintenance staff. The list really is endless. The majority of our children, possibly all our children, will, in addition to their personal or domestic involvement with technology, be actively concerned with it in their careers and they will need to know what it is, how to deal with it, what its costs are, and what its effects are.

Whilst we must accept this educational responsibility as well-rounded, broad and outward looking, there is no need for us as individuals, with our own special interests, enthusiasms and expertise to feel that these, our personal strengths, are not the very foundations of our relations with children who naturally wish to become adult and are only too thankful to find a section of the school staff able to help them engage in what is so obviously a man-sized and useful job. Craft teachers have an enormous advantage over many of our colleagues and it would be a pity to throw it away.

Children, through everyday life and through television, are well aware of the work of engineers. A new city motorway, a gigantic office block, Concorde, lunar modules, are obviously the work of engineers; they have been created by man. The details of the processes of creation are naturally obscure but children see that, by some wonderful means, men have actually achieved these remarkable devices. Other technological marvels are more taken in the stride and not easily recognized as such. Even television is now accepted as almost a part of the natural world. Direct relays of programmes, via satellites, from the other side of the world do not strike the consciousness as being any more remarkable than if the transmissions were to come from a studio in London. Perhaps it would do us all good to be reminded of the basic necessity for there to be engineers, in the background, to see to the smooth functioning of all our services which are too easily taken for granted.

As craft teachers we can readily help pupils to engage in activities which can be seen as being very similar to the real work of our engineers. The foundation of the philosophy of the craftsman is that he exists to create answers to the problems and needs of people as individuals and that into his answers he can build beauty, permanence and excellence in such a way that the individual for whom he has worked derives pleasure and satisfaction from the appreciation of these qualities. The craftsman is, therefore, very close in philosophy and purpose to the engineer. Perhaps the main difference between the two lies in scale. The engineer usually attempts to meet the needs of the masses rather than the exclusive individual. Sometimes his work is ostentatious in that, like the craftsman, his excellence of work is apparent and calls for acclamation – the high performance sports car, the biggest suspension bridge, the fastest computer. Sometimes, and this is probably the more usual, it is self-effacing, hidden and unobtrusive and yet contributes to essential services – the town water supply and sewage systems, the telephone system, – all essential to keep our society, and economy functioning at all.

Practical implications of technology

I now want to focus on the practical aspects of what I have said so far. The argument goes like this:

1 Teachers aim to help children become creative individuals in whatever fields are most appropriate in terms of interest, aptitudes, knowledge and attitudes.

2 Craft teachers are ideally placed to achieve this aim.

3 It follows that craft teachers, in addition to their personal and individual craft strength, must be sympathetic to all sorts of other practical activities which might help any child to become a more creative individual.

4 If this last step in the argument is accepted, then there are two positive outcomes. Firstly the range of possible solutions to very traditional design problems will be broadened to include less familiar but equally acceptable practical activities. Secondly, the range of problems acceptable to school technical departments becomes much broader. It is these two conclusions which calls for a greater involvement of technology in the craft departments of the schools and which I will now examine in more detail, illustrating possibilities and yet warning of dangers.

Technology broadens the range of possible solutions

In the real world of engineering this point might be best illustrated by referring to bridges. In general terms, up until two hundred years ago, the largest span that could carry vehicular traffic was about 150 feet. Broader rivers required multiple span, arch bridges. The advances in iron and steel-making technology made it possible for the ancient suspension principle to be employed for road bridges. Possible spans immediately shot up to 300 feet and have been rising, with the advances in technology, ever since.

Another obvious illustration lies in road and rail transport. For the best part of a century, steam power held a monopoly in rail traction. The advent of electrical machines and the internal combustion engine broke the steam monopoly and even now there is no clear advantage for one form of traction system over another.

The reproduction of music raises an interesting study of how technology broadens the range of possible solution. First it was a question of how to make a musical instrument play automatically. The musical box, polyphon, barrel organ and player piano are examples of how this was done, and what might be regarded as the ultimate, the reproducer piano of the 1920s, complete with electrical power, is a miracle of technological ingenuity. Then came the possibility of recording a performance and reproducing it acoustically without the need for the original instrument itself to be made to play. The succession of developments, which have been based on what has been technologically possible at the particular point in time, is well known. The early cylinder recordings with acoustic reproduction gave way to electrical systems on discs which have reached their present superior capabilities. But the magnetic recorder has also been developing in the last thirty years and to such an extent that discs no longer have a monopoly and now the reproduction systems available can be selected to meet specific individual needs.

Interpreting this into the school workshop situation, perhaps the most obvious example of broadening the range of possible solutions to design problems is with the advance of new materials. Plastics no longer allow wood and metal to have sole rights. Boats, canoes and dinghies, furniture and even buildings can now be built with G.R.P. or other plastic form. It is important to remember that these new materials do not simply provide alternative media in which to create old designs. Rather they provide the opportunity to create completely new forms and designs to meet old design problems.

But new materials are not all. A technological approach to materials can produce completely new visions of how familiar materials might be used more effectively, both on their own and in association with other materials. An understanding of the properties and characteristics of reinforced materials, concrete, plastics, and timber make possible more original solutions to constructional problems. Children frequently require the knowhow to create intensely load-bearing or force-resisting components. The construction of boats, and articles such as oars and paddles can be very seriously limited without this knowledge.

Technology broadens the range of types of design problem acceptable in schools

How many times, I wonder, have boys who have been told to 'think of something to make in wood!' (or metal), come unstuck because there is no object which they really need which could possibly be made in wood, and so have fallen back on a standard version of a coffee table, book trough or table lamp copied from one of the excellent picture books available. I appreciate of course that this itself is a good way of whetting the appetite and discovering the pleasure of successfully working in wood as a medium.

There are two ways in which pupils might use technology to extend the fields in which they can practice creative design. Both are valid under relevant circumstances, but in the wrong circumstances each may do much more harm than good. The first way might be called 'black box' technology. Here, pupils and, quite likely, teachers accept that the precise and blind following of detailed instructions, without knowledge of their fundamental meaning, may enable something to be built which works very well. Making a hi-fi amplifier by following the details given in a popular magazine; constructing a hovercraft or a linear induction motor to purchased plans; making a go-kart with prescribed steering geometry; these, and very many more, are examples of technology broadening the range of craft activities from the text book approach of standard wood and metal work jobs. This approach has its uses in that it may well motivate pupils to more creative work in similar fields; it provides knowledge of specific skills and techniques which may be of use in the future. It has its dangers, however, in that the amplifier becomes as identified and stereotyped as the proverbial tea-pot stand; it could develop an almost cavalier attitude towards technology which overlooks the dangers and the potential of technology. It has nevertheless a valuable role to play in the education of some of our less imaginative (not less able) pupils.

The second approach is the fundamental approach. It means using technological fields such as mechanics, electronics, aeronautics and control, in which to engage pupils in the design work itself. It has been shown that even average-ability pupils are capable of designing to some extent in these fields, even if there is also a 'black box' element sometimes present.

Conclusion

In summing up, I want to reiterate my opening remarks about the interdependence of art, craft and technology especially as they relate to school creative activities. If our aim is to help children to identify and accept problem situations capable of being resolved by creative personal design activities, then we must develop in our children the capacities to analyze problem situations, synthesize possible solutions, optimize, and realize a design in practical form. We must develop in our children a knowledge of technological methods and resources, including the capacity to continue the acquisition of such resources as time goes by; a sensitivity towards the aesthetic aspects of design solution; and lastly, but not least, the capacity to turn idealized designs into a practical three dimensional form which meets all the requirements of function, reliability and accuracy.

These points will, I hope, convince all of us of the wide range of qualities needed and of the respect the artist, the craftsman and the engineer must have for each other. Let us avoid the 'three culture' stigma being attached to craft teachers. Let us respect and applaud the contributions our colleagues make.

10

Design education — with research and development in mind

K. JENNINGS

Keith Jennings is Head of the Design Faculty at Weston Favell Upper School, Northampton. He received his initial training at Redland College Bristol and recently completed a B. Phil (Education) degree at Birmingham University. A member of the Institute of Craft Education since 1963 he has held office at local and at national level and is currently the Northampton Conference Chairman and has been nominated for the Presidency in 1977.

Abstract   This paper looks at the present trend of combining design subjects, and outlines the need to review the aims and objectives of the subjects taught and the methods by which they are taught. The need for a systematic approach to instruction is canvassed and current theories of learning are analysed and questions raised regarding the futility of research whose findings are educationally acceptable yet rarely applied in the school situation. The point is made that a system must be devised to enable a debate to ensue, which will reconcile theoretical views with the practicalities and allow curriculum development to proceed with less of the 'hit and miss' approach that has been, hitherto, all too frequent.

Recently there has been a growing desire to integrate traditional subjects within the secondary school curriculum. Such subjects as art, home economics, metalwork, needlework, technical drawing and woodwork have been included in these developments. These traditional areas, together with the newer educational subject areas of ceramics, motor-vehicle engineering, photography, plastics, social crafts, technology, television and others, have, in recent years been combined to form faculties. These large units are frequently called 'design departments', 'creative studies departments', 'expressive arts faculties' and numerous other names which define an area of the curriculum that utilizes both two- and three-dimensional materials.

Many such departments have been created for a variety of reasons, but all too rarely because groups of teachers have felt a need to co-ordinate their activities. Many education authorities seem to support the idea of creating firmer links between art, the crafts and home economics and this commitment has seen large-scale building programmes which have produced open-plan or semi-open plan suites which house the multitude of practical resources. In many cases the planners omitted to consider that teachers destined to work in such areas would need re-training and it is only recently that initial and in-service training is beginning to cope with the problems that have been created by building schemes which have out-paced the rate of adequate teacher education.

The establishment of a design department must automatically mean a new approach to the teaching-learning situation and also to the techniques of organization and management of such an educational unit. The major opportunity, without question, is for a fresh look to be taken at the aims and objectives of design education, its place within the total school curriculum and the methods which educators might use. A realistic approach to such curriculum development has been provided by Bloom. He suggests that the needs of the students should be analyzed and the curriculum designed to provide the skills and knowledge necessary for a useful adult life:

> Whatever the case in the past, it is very clear that in the middle of the 20th century we find ourselves in a rapidly changing and unpredictable culture. It seems almost impossible to foresee the particular ways in which it will change in the near future or the particular problems which will be paramount in five or ten years. Under these conditions, much emphasis must be placed in the schools on the development of generalized ways of attacking problems and on knowledge which can be applied to a wide range of new situations. That is, we have the task of preparing individuals

for problems that cannot be foreseen in advance, and about all that can be done under such conditions is to help the student acquire generalized intellectual abilities and skills which will serve him well in many new situations.[1]

Taberner[2] suggests that the importance of Bloom's statement is that the emphasis is on a process-centred curriculum as distinct from a content-centred approach to learning. An approach which is process-centred relies on the student developing skills which enable him to acquire, manipulate and apply knowledge, as opposed to setting the student the chore of absorbing factual information for regurgitation under examination conditions.

If courses are to be designed to facilitate meaningful learning, teachers too, must acquire skills to cope with the changing demands of the educational system within which they operate. Rowntree describes these special skills as the domain of educational technology:

> It is concerned with the design and evaluation of curricula and learning experiences and with the problems of implementing and renovating them. Essentially, it is a rational, problem-solving approach to education, a way of thinking sceptically and systematically about learning and teaching.[3]

This systematic approach to education problem solving has been well described in numerous articles. Mager wrote:

> Once an instructor decides he will teach his students something, several kinds of activity are necessary on his part if he is to succeed. He must first decide upon the goals he intends to reach at the end of his course. He must then select procedures, content, and methods that are relevant to the objectives, cause the student to interact with appropriate subject matter *in accordance with principles of learning*; and finally, measure or evaluate the students performance according to the objectives or goals originally selected.[4]

How often do teachers rely upon 'hit and miss' judgment as a basis for curriculum development rather than referring to the accepted principles of learning that Mager mentions? What are the current theories and what relevance have they?

Romiszowski[5] reports that recent approaches to the theory of learning have digressed from the path which seeks to utilize the same technique for all learning, towards a technique where the instruction is matched to the problems that present themselves. Work such as that of Skinner, Gilbert, Mager and Bloom laid a foundation upon which the learning theories of Ausubel, Bruner, Piaget, Miller and Gagné have been built.

Gilbert reorganized many of the ideas put forward by other members of the behaviourist school and presented them as a guide for the design of instruction. In his publication *Mathetics − The Technology of Education*[6] he lays down rules for the analysis of various learning tasks and ways by which appropriate training exercises can be devised. Much of his work was derived from reasoning rather than experimentation, although many of his ideas have been confirmed by recent experiments. His classification of learning tasks into chains, discriminations and generalizations are still of value today. Many critics of Gilbert's *Mathetics* suggest that his model does not cater for creative behaviour and it could well be that they find the work of Gagné[7] more acceptable.

Gagné describes a hierarchical model which contains eight major kinds of learning, each of which has a different set of conditions for its optimal occurrence. The eight kinds are called signal learning, stimulus-response learning, motor and verbal chaining, multiple discriminations, concept learning, rule learning and problem solving. Although all types of learning may require certain general conditions for their establishment such as those of contiguity, repetition and reinforcement, the specific conditions for the establishment of concepts rules and principles, according to Gagné, are in addition to these. Gagné's other major principle is that of cumulative learning, which states that the learning of any new capability builds upon prior learning. According to this theory, there is a specifiable minimal prerequisite for each new learning task. If the learner is unable to recall this prerequisite capability, or one similar, he is unable, it is claimed, to learn the new task.

Mager's model relies on the definition of learning which suggests that it is a change in behaviour or a capacity for new behaviour. He asserts that teachers would be wise to define the aims and objectives of their lessons in terms of the behaviour patterns they wish to establish. This implies a student orientated, learning orientated approach, rather than one based on subject matter coverage. It is a useful model because once an objective is defined in behavioural terms then it is not too difficult to design an appropriate test to evaluate the teaching. Mager would claim that the problem is not so much in stating the objective as in stating the correct one. His theory was initially formulated for programmed instruction methods, but this was soon applied to the design of all instructional applications. He outlined the components of a behavioural objective as

1 a statement of what the student should be able to do at the end of the learning session
2 the conditions under which he should be able to exhibit the terminal behaviour
3 the standard to which he should be able to perform.

Bloom outlines general aims and more detailed objectives, and categorizes three types of objectives:

1 cognitive objectives — what the student should know or be able to do
2 affective objectives — what the student should feel and be prepared to do
3 psychomotor objectives — physical skills that the student should develop.

Bloom's classification of objectives are arranged in a hierarchy in which the lower levels are prerequisite to the higher levels. His categories in the cognitive domain (knowledge, comprehension, application, analysis, synthesis and evaluation) are levels of students' thought processes and have to be taken into consideration alongside Gagné's conditions under which different types of learning occur.

Miller[8] contends that for any effective sequence of instruction there must be four provisions. He considers that they are motivation, cue, response and reward. They are relevant to the learning of all kinds of students, and presumably to all kinds of learning tasks. It is, however, questionable whether these principles are ever violated, even in the most traditional institutions, because the skilled teacher would claim them to be obvious.

The views of Skinner[9] on instruction, offer no great disagreement with Miller's. Their increased specificity, however, centre around the principle of stimulus control, or the ways in which reinforcement can be used to establish both more precise, and more elaborate learning by manipulation of the stimuli impinging on the learner. Skinner offers some specific suggestions for the design of instruction and gives practical procedures for shaping motor responses, for establishing discriminations by successive approximations of stimuli, and for chaining together the steps in complex procedures. For a number of learning tasks, these procedures are most specific and undoubtedly successful.

Ausubel's model[10] is devised to provide students with meaningful learning as opposed to rote learning. His most important principle is that meaningful learning takes place when a new idea is subsumed into a related structure of already existing knowledge. The result of this process is the acquisition of a new set of meanings. The major implication here is that the learner needs to be provided with a meaningful structure before he attempts to learn a new principle. The second feature of the model is that any subject should be presented by progressive differentiation of content, the most general ideas first and then the more detailed and specific ones. The third principle is highly similar to Gagné's cumulative learning, it is the need to insist on mastery of on-going lessons before new material is introduced. In other words, where new ideas are introduced they need to be deliberately related to old ideas, significant similarities pointed out and apparent inconsistencies reconciled.

Most of these models have common features and add up to a strong specification of how instruction should be organized and presented for most effective learning. They tell an instructional designer what to do first, what sequence of ideas he should continue with, how to ensure remembering, and what kind of final outcomes to expect.

The Schools Council's Science 5 to 13 Project[11] is one of the few recent innovations which has been developed with specific learning theory in mind. The objectives have been classified in stages which conform with the Piagetian description of the mental development of children.

It seems a tragedy that so much time, effort and money is being channelled into research yet few teachers are either aware of its findings or are prepared to implement the information available. The desirability of applying such information will be conceded by many, but the practicalities involved and the constraints against such a possibility ever arising in more than a few progressive schools must be acknowledged with regret. The debate must, however, continue and centre around the question, 'How can research findings and educational theories be implemented?' It must involve some consideration of methods whereby findings can be made more readable and more readily available to a wider audience than at the present time. It must take into account the need to reconcile the theoretical with the practical and the actual with the possible. It must include some discussion on methods whereby the best possible results can be obtained, utilizing the educational resources available and the possibility of adopting a cost-effective approach to the learning process if found necessary.

A recent report[12] analyzing the aims and objectives of craft education went some way towards answering the questions posed in this paper, but many still remain unanswered. The report concluded:

Over the years the subject has moved from Manual Training through Handicraft with its emphasis on the product, to that which is evolving today — studies aimed to promote the personal development of individuals embracing design and technology. These studies still retain a concern for knowledge and skills but as a means to an end. Teachers are becoming aware of the new skills; Communicative, Manipulative, Exploratory, Discriminatory, Verbal and Constructional. When the aims are understood teachers will be better able to formulate teaching and enabling objectives which suit local situations and the confusion which may have been experienced in recent years about the role of craft education may be diminished in the process. The subject is compounded of many parts of many disciplines and skills and offers the outlet for the basic human need to create. *There is scope for a great variety of teaching talent* and expertise, success cannot be measured by examinations or by techniques but can be recognized by the quality and calibre of the end product, the individual.

By not utilizing *all* the teaching talent and expertise available we are in a situation of not doing the best for our pupils and are failing to optimize the teaching and learning process which society has a right to demand.

References
1 Bloom B.J. *A Taxonomy of Educational Objectives,* Longman (17th ed. 1972)
2 Taberner D. 'Design Education', *Craft Education,* No. 36 (1974)
3 Rowntree D. *Educational Technology in Curriculum Development,* Harper & Row (1974)
4 Mager R.F. *Preparing Instructional Objectives,* Fearon Publishers (1961)

5 Romiszowski A.J. *The Selection and Use of Instructional Media,* Kogan Page (1974)
6 Gilbert T.F. 'Mathetics — The Technology of Education' *Journal of Mathetics,* Nos 1 & 2 (1961)
7 Gagné R.M. *The Conditions of Learning,* Holt, Rinehart & Winston (1973)
8 Miller N.E. Graphic Communication and the Crisis in Education *A V Communication Review* (1957)
9 Skinner B.F. *Cumulative Record,* Methuen (1961)
10 Ausubel D.P. and Robinson F.G. *School Learning,* Holt, Rinehart & Winston (1973)
11 Schools Council 'Science 5 to 13: Objectives for Children Learning Science'
12 Conference of Handicraft Advisers 'A Report on Craft Education' (1972)

11
Engendering genius

E. OGILVIE

Dr Eric Ogilvie is Director of Nene College. He was Director of a Schools Council Project on creative thinking and the teaching of gifted children which published a report in 1973. He is currently Director of another Schools Council project concerned with the construction of learning kits for gifted children. Dr Ogilvie is an occasional broadcaster on radio and television, is a consultant to the Open University and acts as examiner for CNAA Degrees.

Abstract This paper discusses the influence of confusing beliefs and parental and teacher expectations on the educative aspects of creative activity. It proposes guidelines to the recognition of creative ability and considers the need for a change in attitude and direction related to developmental and sociological issues.

When I view the current situation in our schools I am reminded of a tale by Harry Benjamin which runs something as follows:

> There was once a school in the woods devoted to rearing all the animals in accordance with the principles of democratic equality and thus to providing every youngster above all else with a good general education. A teacher in the school devised a well thought out curriculum comprising all the most useful activities that her pupils might need in later life — Running, Jumping, Climbing and Flying — and proceeded vigorously to encourage all the animals to become proficient in everything. The squirrel was something of a star pupil — indeed he got straight 'A's in everything except Flying, in which he really was not very good. The teacher, observing this relative weakness, immediately turned her attention to devising remedial exercises, as every good teacher should, and started, very logically, with having the squirrel practise jumping take-offs. The squirrel was a diligent pupil: he worked hard and practised endlessly. Despite his total lack of progress, the teacher reminded him of the old adage about 'If at first you don't succeed', and because she was a good teacher, fully convinced of the need for every pupil to have a balanced education, she contrived to help the little squirrel to renew his enthusiasm. He continued to practise take-offs with more energy than before. He tried and he tried.
>
> Alas! The squirrel's efforts were fruitless and he gradually realized that he was a failure. Nor was his failure now confined only to Flying. The take-off exercises overdone, his legs stiffened, his motivation weakened, soon his straight 'A's in Running, Jumping and Climbing had become 'D's. Reluctantly the teacher concluded that the squirrel's early promise was an illusion and relegated him to the 'opportunity' class for specialist attention.

Ultimately, no doubt, our squirrel ended up in the hands of a psychologist as an unintelligent, nervous wreck but we need continue this story no further. The point, I hope, is made. It is not that teachers are fools. It is simply to draw attention to the fact that we parents and teachers are all obsessed with the idea of a balanced education; a concept so inimical to the elicitation of talent that it ought to be under constant attack. Whoever became really outstanding without demonstrating a powerful, almost unreasonable imbalance in his interests? Who, in our complex society of today, with its multiplicity of different activities and its sum total of knowledge expanding geometrically, can hope to achieve beyond the great majority of his fellows without conscious and deliberate specialization? It is time we realized that what is needed in education has nothing to do with 'balance' but everything to do with 'integration': it is not the boring mediocrity and sameness of the so-called balanced personality that marks out the budding genius but rather the lively individuality which characterizes the 'unbalanced', yet highly integrated youngster: and it is the environmental conditions associated with the development of the latter that require our attention.

Expectations of excellence

Clearly the attitudes of adults are fundamental elements in any child-rearing environment and adult expectations of children will govern all else. It is thus a most unhappy fact that parents are brainwashed into thinking that their own children cannot possibly become gifted. Unless they are cranks, parents on the whole are particularly humble people: they do not wish to be seen as attempting to gain undeserved personal kudos through their children nor do they wish to hold unrealistic expectations regarding what their own progeny might achieve. Teachers are in a somewhat similar case, with the added difficulty that they are frequently taught in college courses that a readily recognizable stereotype of the gifted child exists and that he (never she!) is a very rare bird indeed. The possibility that any individual teacher's own class might contain a budding Einstein, Churchill, Nasser, Picasso, or Menhuin is thus seen to be so remote that few teachers dare even to consider it, much less draw the attention of others to outstanding children in their classes: and this is true even when they come across children who, by learning to speak and read early, fit the traditional stereotype fairly well! With a child who seems merely to be possessed of powerful and biased interests rather than some sort of general verbal ability, there is almost no chance whatsoever that the presence of potentially outstanding talent will be suspected. On the contrary, such a child will be looked upon as foolish, or queer, and every effort will be made to force him to become 'a generalist', just like our little squirrel in the forest.

Here then is a mighty stumbling block to the evocation and development of talent on any significant scale. The very people who have the best opportunity to recognize and respond effectively to budding genius steadfastly refuse to look for it in the children they themselves know well. If talent is to flower then it must do so despite rather than because of the activities of parents and teachers. How is it that we are so foolish? How does it come about that we have so pessimistic a view of the creative potential of human beings? The situation is complex and no doubt there are many reasons but several stand out; firstly we believe that genetic predestination enmeshes us all and that only the very few are born with an ability to achieve greatness. Secondly, we seldom, if ever, question the truth and utility of the concept of intelligence or innate general cognitive capacity and thus become fundamentally elitist in all our thinking about all educational matters. Thirdly, we are blinded by the current educational dogma concerning the nature of creative activity and the conditions under which it flourishes. And finally, we seem deep down to be absolutely convinced that giftedness will out sooner or later however adverse the early or late environment in which the potential genius finds itself: some go so far as to argue that the so called gifted are already sufficiently advantaged for us not to worry about them and even that it might be fairer to handicap them a bit lest they find life too easy and lacking in the struggle which faces the rest of us and is apparently so character-building.

Uncreative creativity

Each of these points requires expansion elsewhere and for the present discussion must be confined to a very brief consideration of the nature of creative activity. The term 'creativity' is bandied about by some in such a manner as to cause us to wonder, somewhat cynically, whether the main reason for its use is to hide under its prestigious umbrella a huge pile of readily produced rubbish. The unrestricted and uncritical verbal suppurations of well-intentioned youngsters are welcomed as 'creative writing'. The careless rapturings manifest in random splashings of a well plucked paintbrush on a grubby piece of old newsprint elicit eulogistic commentaries accompanied by cries of wonder at the spontaneity and novelty of the product. The disconnected diatribe which is frequently the banal outcome of what purports to be creative drama receives a degree of acclaim not nowadays accorded even to the works of Shakespeare himself.

There is some over-generalization here, no doubt, but there is hardly exaggeration. It is not so long ago that a primate won a national painting competition and that a well-mounted piece of bark was recognized as 'creative art'. There is little wonder then that parents and teachers feel no need to have defined expectations of what children might achieve when the products of genius are apparently so effortlessly created and monkeys can do better than men. Unfortunately they are not the only people who have stopped asking how far the school system provides, and ought to provide, abundant opportunity for the growth of talent of every kind. Economists[1], blinded by short run static models of the economy, gleefully endeavour to convince us that investment in education pays neither society nor the individual, and that cash is best diverted elsewhere. It is maddeningly odd that these same economists will strenuously support a search for oil-wells when fewer than one in ten drillings are successful and yet will cavalierly disregard the fact that the only self-generative and hence permanently expanding source of wealth lies not in natural but in human hydrocarbons. One single discovery by some talented chemist, physicist or what have you could put the world's oil men out of business over night: alternatively he could make every drop of oil we use go ten times as far[2]. It is not that economists have got their calculations wrong, it is simply that until the school system ensures that no child is ever held back, current economic arithmetic is totally irrelevant. It is part of a vicious cycle wherein the product is seen as incapable of improvement and cost effectiveness can therefore only be achieved by contraction; and yet, given the prevalence of attitudes so plainly inimical to investment in human resources it is surely not surprising that despite all the efforts of enthusiastic teachers our schools are characterized not by open-ended opportunities and the urgent encouragement of potential talent but rather by an all pervading system of brakes and obstacles. Most of us who know the system well would agree that practically all children are held back to some extent, and perhaps the most energetic are held back most of all. Certainly none but the extremely handicapped child is treated as an individual in any real sense: all are placed in groups and subjected to lock-step curricula based on traditional expectations often enshrined in out-dated text books and methods of instruction.

A reduction in the pupil/teacher ratio of itself will not ensure improvement. And to that extent the economists are probably right; at the same time an increase in the pupil/teacher ratio will unquestionably ensure that massive wastage occurs. The plain fact is that we need more teachers but it is at the same time essential for us to become far more aware of other hindrances to pupil's progress beyond that presented by insufficient access to the teacher. It is immediately clear, for example that no teacher can be outstandingly good in every field of endeavour and yet this is what we expect of our primary teachers. They are supposed to be omniscient polymaths who can be all things to all children all the time. Can it really be true that no young child ever goes beyond his or her teacher in mathematics, art, music or soccer? If that is true then surely the brakes on talent are even greater than we are surmising. It can of course be argued that any teacher can easily enable a particular child to go beyond the teacher's own achievements in some field and there is a grain of truth in that, but at the same time it needs to be stressed that everything depends upon the supplementary learning resources available, and that even with an otherwise good teacher in the best of present circumstances the levels of expectation which govern what a teacher requires of his or her children must be heavily dependent upon his or her own personal achievements in the given area. Where these are low then teacher expectations are likely to be low and children's achievements even lower. Putting the matter bluntly: non-craft teachers are unlikely to worry if the young craftsmen in their classes do not race ahead and go beyond them if only because they are unaware of the possibilities within the reach of such children. It might even be that some teachers would be glad if circumstances prevented too rapid progress by their most outstanding pupils.

A Tropopause curriculum
Let us suppose that our children are fortunate: that they are somehow given access to a group of teachers rather than one and that these teachers together represent a range of expertise. Let us further suppose that our children are not grouped in 'streams' or 'sets' and are thus freed from an immediate need to move at the pace of the slowest ship in the convoy. Can we then be satisfied that every child will move in any and every direction which he and we regard as interestingly worthwhile without let or hindrance? Not necessarily: no teacher can give individual attention for any significant length of time to thirty children. If he eschews class lessons as he should it will still be the case that the children are faced with a 'tropopause' curriculum: that is a curriculum whereby they will be guided through books and work cards which embody hidden but nonetheless low ceilings. They will never rise beyond the tropopause, or what in English junior schools might be called the 'Book 4 barrier'. Book 5 awaits Willy in secondary school and little Willy must mark time until he gets there, regardless of his progress in the meantime. It is true that if he is fortunate he may be presented with what is called an 'enrichment programme' but the richness of so-called enrichment programmes as currently available is highly questionable. Nonetheless some will say that all is well so long as little Willy has abundant opportunity for experimenting endlessly and for expressing himself without restraint. The purposefulness of his experimenting and the quality of his self-expression are, we are told, quite irrelevant and our greatest fear should be of in some way constraining and oppressing little Willy and thus killing his budding creativity.

In fact the truth lies elsewhere. Too much stress can be placed on freedom and notably on freedom from the restraints which are inevitably involved in the recognition of standards of excellence. One reason may be a failure to appreciate the logical fact that before we can start to do much towards creating conditions under which talent will flourish, or even begin to recognize people who might come to possess it, we must first be prepared to distinguish those products which manifestly reflect and require talent from those which do not. If we are not prepared to assay this admittedly difficult task, then we should join the ranks of the de-schoolers. If we fear the wolves so much, we should not enter the forest, and I at least respect those who, frightened of being burnt, stay out of the kitchen. I cannot however join their ranks. I believe that despite notable mistakes we can and do distinguish the better from the worse, the more developmental from the less, and the truly expressive from the truly oppressive. I believe that even now we can at least formulate tentative guidelines for recognizing products which demonstrate talent and thence imply the conditions for evoking and developing it.

What might such guidelines comprehend? It would be an arrogance for one man to

63

assume that he knew all the answers but the following proposals might be thought worthy of consideration: there might possibly be general agreement that no product worthy of recognition as demonstrating real ability will (i) be effortlessly produced at a first attempt, (ii) be capable of replication by any but the highly skilled and technically competent, (iii) fail to call upon a battery of skills and techniques which are themselves consequent upon training, careful application over periods of time, and maintainable only by constant practice.

In interpreting these guidelines our expectations in regard to age will need careful and constant revision as has been implied earlier, and to emphasize these characteristics is not to denigrate novelty, originality, spontaneity, or even serendipity. But novelty, originality and spontaneity by themselves cannot be the critical criteria for recognizing a product as worthy of the term 'creative'. In any event only the expert can really judge the degree of novelty possessed by any particular element or event. As for serendipity, there is no doubt that only the highly skilled and knowledgeable are likely to distinguish the few significant accidental juxtapositions from the myriads of consequent and concomitant but unrelated and insignificant events which occur throughout all life. However exciting or attention-demanding the chaotic and accidental might be it is at best of momentary consequence and has little to do with the conditions under which talent will flourish.

Masters and Masterpieces

The implications of the above are manifold and must be fully worked out elsewhere. I have suggested that obstacles to the development of talent abound in current child-rearing practices and that the fundamental attitudes and ideas upon which these practices are based must be changed as a first step if we are to be certain that in the future full many a flower is seen to blossom abundantly. I have indicated the nature of the obstacles within the system especially in relation to our failure to individualize learning and our refusal to define ever-improving standards in the quality of all that we encourage children to do. I have stressed that without masterpieces there can be no masters, and without masters there will certainly be no masterpieces. Engendering genius then depends upon our willingness constantly to inject new energies into the benign spiral created when a master, having produced his own masterpiece, enables apprentices to go beyond him and takes the greatest delight in their work when that happens.

I would conclude by thanking the Institute and College of Craft Education for the opportunity to express these views on the occasion of their Northampton Conference 1976. Our greatest enemy is an apathy borne of satisfaction with the status quo and we need not be over fearful whilst the Institute remains active. Standards of excellence, like democracy, require our eternal vigilance.

References

1 Merrett A.J., p.2, *Times Educational Supplement,* 25 July 1975
2 'Britain Leads Second Green Revolution' (concerning work at Rothamstead), *Daily Telegraph,* 15 August 1975

12

Out on a limb

J. ORTON

John Orton is Director of Creative Arts at Kingsthorpe Upper School, Northampton. He is a member of the Council of the National Association for Design Education. He was previously Head of the Craft Department at Grange School, Oldham.

Abstract   This paper explores basic educational considerations related to the role and aspirations of a craftsman/teacher. It comments pertinently on changes in facilities, organization and approach and gives an informal personal forecast of the future.

Bernard Aylward in his recent address to the Design in General Education summer school at the Royal College of Art referred to the bombardment of change that teachers have experienced during the last few years. Changes that have often put the teacher out on a limb, changes often without support. One of the changes Mr Aylward referred to was the change in facilities. I have worked for eight years in what have become known, perhaps misleadingly, as design departments. This work has involved me in many other changes, changes in teacher status, curriculum and syllabus, changes in methods and attitudes.

I trained as a silversmith, but after ATD I found it perhaps easier to sustain my own and the children's interest by teaching general art. For the first six or seven years, I became a very ordinary art teacher − eventually with my own department. My main concern at that time was with my own studio, my own groups, looking for good ideas to copy and trying, fairly successfully, to provide the largest number of outlets, everything from pottery to photography, in one studio and a stockroom. I suppose my main attribute at that time was an unswerving faith in my own ability which would have made any self-analysis of what I was doing distorted to say the least.

I outline this background because it may be similar to that of many teachers then and since who have gained the promotion described below.

The position at the Oldham school was described as head of an integrated craft department. The previous head of department had left after the facilities had been open for twelve months. I was surprised and delighted to be accepted for the position. On preliminary visits to the school, I was relieved to find the existing staff in the department to be even more confused and apprehensive than myself. The department's open-plan facilities shared the first building of a new comprehensive school with the science department. The staff's apprehension was perhaps well justified, and similar feelings must have been shared by teachers working in other authorities which have launched design departments. This apprehension must always be hypothetical; I wonder how much of it disappears in a working situation. In my own case, colleagues were expected to cope with large open-plan, well-equipped facilities, having moved from a small secondary modern school on which the new comprehensive was to be founded. In their previous situation, they had shared little professional contact. Where were they to look for a lead? They had a supposedly super-charged head of department who was determined to carry out his brief (at least I had a brief) to form integrated links, weld the staff into a team and suddenly conjure bigger and better things from them. I do not know how super-charged I was or how well qualified I was. How well qualified was anyone eight years ago? Are qualifications for a role such as this obtainable today outside of getting in and gaining the experience? Eight years ago I knew nothing of home economics, yet I was firmly determined to integrate the subject with all the others facilitated in my new department. I knew very little about compiling timetables, but whilst 3C came to the department for seven periods and 3A for four, I was determined that they should share the same courses. I quickly saw the need for block timetabling, boys and girls sharing the same work in mixed-ability groups.

My early convictions about these conditions have changed slightly. My brief to form a team was perhaps the hardest to fulfil. Colleagues had formed relationships in their previous school, some good, some deeply divided. I was the newcomer, even the 'interloper'. I managed to exchange a very few words with one lady during the whole of the first year. There was an almost overwhelming variety of attitudes, even amongst the staff in my new department. I knew nothing of man-management and if I gained any skills in that direction, I have learned them the hard way. There have been times when I have been tempted to turn my back completely on unproductive relationships. My only answer was that the encouragement for all views to be aired during meetings would augment the involvement of everyone in discussion; but this is not the complete answer, there will always be those who are incapable or apathetic about making a contribution.

Our first and biggest mistake and one which persisted for some time was to attempt to keep traditional roles and subjects going, embarking on an inevitable variety of basic circus, followed by options. We designed the circus roundabout in a variety of ways, short and sweet tastes of each subject, constant movement. I have the feeling that I was the only one in the department not confused. Up went the cry that nothing was being finished properly; my goodness, the materials that we went through. We tried longer periods of time in each subject. In this situation, the child after leaving a session of woodwork, for example, might not sample the situation again for up to twelve months. Obviously, this was not the best organization for continuity. At the end of the first three years came options between the traditional subjects and syllabus-based-on-examination subjects; integration stopped.

I think this is the crux of many a dilemma in organizing integrated or (as I prefer to call them) combined courses. Can the specialist expect to keep his subject intact? Can he expect to keep his traditional role? The answer must be a personal one and the individual may honestly find adaptation unjustified by changes in approach that may be advocated. I believe in an area where we are dealing with materials to encourage creativity, to teach skills, gather experience and knowledge in materials and above all develop interest and curiosity, there is no justification at any stage in secondary education to condemn the child to one member of staff, let alone one material area, even though the present examination system will often call for this. A combined approach calls for rethinking and re-shaping the secondary course to form a basic part of every child's education, with no opting out or restriction because of the demands of other subject areas. Tangible and understandable core subject material must be provided, so that each specialist can consider his individual contribution to develop the core.

In my own experience, options at fourteen plus have always been frustrating and never satisfactory. The basic pretext for options is the need to specialize. I believe in providing flexible courses at this level — courses that allow for a study in depth if this suits the individual's requirement, but which will also allow wide ranging use of materials for the characters who can cope and benefit from this.

The early years in the integrated situation left my colleagues and myself with experience of various types of circus or roundabout, and an unsatisfactory feeling about our specialist option system. The ill-effects of our early attempts at drawing together came from the complicated organization needed. Perhaps I did not realize the ill effects quickly enough being at the centre, and perhaps, to be honest, I thought things had to be complicated to be impressive. One consequence of any complicated organization is that staff can be unsure of the basic situation and of themselves. This can lead a desire to opt out or they will develop a reliance upon others to imitate proceedings. Drawing together into a team situation means a lot of preparation and the very least that there must be is communication between members of the team. Again, creating an impression of hard work and involvement can lead to over-preparation. Work cards, slides, tapes are all very impressive, but so much time can be spent in their preparation but they cannot in themselves ensure a successful lesson. Success can only come with imagination and inventiveness on the teacher's part in the classroom, perhaps more so in a team situation. If two or even three teachers have confidence and respect for each other in the classroom, the benefits can be far-reaching for the children and for the teachers themselves. Unfortunately, not all staff can fit into this situation. But even in the situation where the department may have only one woodwork or pottery specialist, creating a piece of work in either media can benefit at various stages from consultation with other teachers, and the teachers can benefit from each other.

As I said, being in the centre of things, it took a while to realize the overwhelming effects of complicated subjects organization. We tried to keep the traditional subjects continuing in what we felt was an integrated situation, but the subjects became so diluted as to prove ineffectual, and the demands of each subject (although very often duplicated) could not be satisfied. I think the choice is clear between the traditional way of separating boys' subjects (metalwork or woodwork) from girls' subjects (needlework or home economics — with art or technical drawing tucked in on the timetable if we are lucky) and the modern method of integrating all pupils in combined subjects. Some form of combined course must be more beneficial as part of a liberal and general education. It must be wrong to cut off young and hopefully enquiring minds from any of the opportunities, facilities and staff expertise at any stage in secondary school. If this is the main reason for having a combined course, the structure for such a course should allow the child continual access to all facilities, materials and to all the specialist staff involved.

Towards the close of my time at Oldham and in my present school, the team I work with have attempted to work out the lowest common denominators among the traditional specialist subjects, the driving forces which pre-empt all we do in our area of the curriculum. The common driving forces have become the basis of new subject areas. These subjects override the traditional, but can only exist with combined contributions from traditional specialist teachers. The results' seem obvious to me in the light of experience and I hope that they will not seem too contrived to the reader.

The first subject area is based very loosely on solving problems in materials which perhaps we wrongly call design. Problem solving is too simple a phrase to cover the thinking behind this area. We prefer the problems to come from the children; for them to work at the problem, more than one material must be available — the knowledge and skill to such materials must have been acquired, and indeed the problem of using the material will be paramount for many children. A certain amount of abstract thinking, planning and testing must be part of this subject and perhaps most important, further knowledge and skill must be sought to overcome the problem. We feel that this enquiry for knowledge should be done individually therefore the problem should be individual, unique to each child, or a clearly defined role of a group project. The problems should be wide-ranging, involving not only wood, metal and plastic but ideally ceramics, fabrics and graphics bound together with the problem-solving approach, research, testing and perhaps working drawings (including technical drawing). The testing and research required may involve experience in technological and scientific techniques. This subject requires experience and learning in all the activities listed above. I feel that the subject can be varied according to the department's strength and weaknesses and even to suit individual teacher's attitudes, preferences and talents, although assessing these constructively can lead to difficulties.

The overriding objective of such a subject of combined course is that the student should experience the problem solving, the design process. In the senior year, the student should be able to concentrate directly on a particular material, with a study in depth. At Kingsthorpe, we have devised a Mode III in CSE and O level to examine the senior part of this combined course and we hope in due course to use it as a natural lead into the Oxford A level course in design.

The second combined course is art. In many design departments, art and design are seen as one, and run as a combined course. I would be the first to agree that many aspects of art and design are indistinguishable. Our reasons for separating them are primarily educational. Whilst acknowledging that design is creative, we feel that the students should be provided with a purely creative outlet in materials without the exacting restrictions design impels. Art calls for a different approach, both from the teacher and the student. Art is a personal response that the teacher needs to stimulate, and here there are dangers in over-stimulating to the extent where the student's response merely becomes an extension of the teacher's imagination. The objective should be to stimulate what is within the student, so that what he creates is an expression of himself, his environment, his experience. Art should allow the student to be sensitive to his own background and through work and shared situations allow him to become sensitive to the creative endeavours of others.

In design, the student's work must be acceptable to other people in a practical sense. We could encourage a student to carry out a sculpture in GRP, or the student might be interested in designing a sculptural shape in GRP capable of supporting the human body whilst relaxing — both, it could be argued are design problems. My feeling is that the first situation should only arise from the development of ideas and feelings where the problem is one of finding and using a suitable material to put those ideas and feelings into visual terms. The development of ideas towards a visual state is purely personal, there is almost complete freedom of interpretation; the limitation will be provided only by the material and the student's skill. (As stated earlier, the main problem for many students will be the use of materials themselves.) The second problem in GRP is extremely exacting and very definite, and research and testing would be needed. The only factor shared by both types of approach to using GRP is the limitations of the material. Anyone who considers knowledge of materials and their use as the most important part of their teaching will find my point of view hard to swallow. I believe that art is the visual evidence of the student's ability to respond and react to whatever inspires and stimulates his creative work and that this is more important than the materials he uses to support that evidence. I try to encourage the widest range of specialist teachers to contribute to the art situation. Obviously not only should the traditional fine artists, such as pottery or graphic specialists, be involved but also teachers with more technical skills who can provide tremendous outlets for creative response.

In both combined courses, teachers should see themselves in a consultative role becoming involved at different stages as the student develops his work. The stage of this involvement will depend on the teachers' strengths and talents. Both courses are linked by an attempt to make the children aware of their own environment, particularly the thinking and the forces that shape the man-made part — an important attempt, I hope, that has nothing to do with what John Betjeman described as 'ghastly good taste'. Our students should come to question those responsible for shaping their environment in terms of its visual impact as well as the social and practical implications involved. Of course, art is used to encourage this visual awareness. The social implications of design and the use of materials link our courses with other areas of the curriculum. We see the practical involvement of the decision-makers who affect the environment as being very important. The development of this part of our work is quite intricate and is far from complete. I feel my colleagues considered this attempt an important part of what we should be trying to do and it links strongly with the third subject area so often found in design departments.

Subject titles can prove so inadequate, especially new subject titles, but they are so important when the student needs to show he has reached a certain standard in something that the world at large must understand. I call the third subject area consumer studies, not a very original title and far from adequate. I must admit that in my present department, while the first two combined courses are progressing well, the consumer studies course still requires a lot of development. Consumer studies is a tremendous subject, we are a consumer society and almost certainly one that must learn to do with less. Basically, most students will eventually pour most of their expenditure and energy into the home environment and the family. It should therefore be an area in which all children should become involved, and this involvement should be practical and constructive, yet detached from the more superficial practicalities such as making a Christmas cake or bathing a plastic doll. Some students have never been involved with very young children, others have never mixed with elderly people; some really enjoy a diet of chips and have five pounds to spend every week; consequently, the approach of this course should have regard to the individual. I visualize the home economics specialist co-ordinating the course, but with direct help from other subject specialists from science and social studies, and with a lot of human resource from outside school.

For the three combined courses block timetabling is needed. In the early years, it is important that the students have continuous contact with each course. Obviously each course should be taken by boys and girls and during the early years, at least, in mixed-ability groups. The only limitation on a mixed-ability approach is that design needs a certain amount of academic ability to cope with the senior part of the course. Art should be a core subject up to sixteen plus. At Kingsthorpe, the students follow the three combined courses, and at fourteen plus, all the children continue with art and choose between design and consumer studies, both of which share basic elements.

Art and design share formal teaching of techniques and basic information. This formal teaching is in the form of a developing programme and is the basis on which individual work is attempted. This also helps to provide a language and a stimulus for individual work. A team approach is used for presentation of this programme; this is particularly useful in comparing materials, their qualities and limitations.

Most of the visitors to my department usually come to look at the facilities; what we are doing with them is a secondary consideration. This I find very disappointing. So often, if our students are doing something worthwhile, it is put down to the wonderful facilities, — this is equally disappointing. Many new design blocks have been built in recent years. Perhaps it is the buildings and the economic advantages of open plan that have pushed forward integration more than anything else. This is a pity. I would like to see a building designed from the point of view of a particular philosophy, and a tried and tested way of teaching. In this area of the curriculum developments have stretched our range of experiences and outlooks almost to the stage of separation. Being out on a limb is very far from the main flow. Only one criterion can be applied to the design of design facilities, — flexibility, so that the place may bear the stamp of the personalities of the teachers who will inhabit the buildings over the years, rather than the personalities of architects or advisers. Teachers are far more important than buildings. I feel that combined courses call for specialists who are completely *au fait* with their crafts and who have a curious and imaginative outlook. Skill in his craft will earn the respect of his colleagues through shared curiosity. Mutual respect is essential in a combined situation. Curiosity will allow the specialist to broaden the pupils' activities. Imagination will bring an individual approach, resulting in a variety of contacts which can only be good for the children, and a flexibility of roles, resulting in a mutual understanding amongst teachers.

My conclusion came after eight years of continual assessment with colleagues of what and how we are teaching. Some colleagues have since come to lead their own departments and no doubt will eventually reach different conclusions from mine. I do not think that there is any danger in this as long as each is confident that the students are better able to cope with and get more out of life through what is being taught. We can learn from each other. This learning would be very limited if we were all to do the same thing. By learning from each other, each out on his own particular limb, we can move forward.

13
What has changed?

A.R. PEMBERTON

Allan R. Pemberton is Senior Adviser in Design for Clwyd Education Authority. He was formerly Senior Research Fellow, Schools Council Design and Craft Project, University of Keele.

Abstract   This paper reviews research and development in design education over the last few years. It elaborates the aims, objectives and findings of the Schools Council Design and Craft Project and shows areas of change resulting from the project.

At a time when all levels of educational provision are becoming more and more accountable, nothing could be more apt than a review of the value and impact of national Schools Council projects. The Design and Craft Project spent time establishing its main purpose and it is only fair to judge outcomes against this. Working Paper 26 offers criteria established at the outset of the main developmental phase; of the intention at that time none could be more important than the statement that

> ... [it is] hoped that the results of the Project will point the way ahead for handicraft teachers and all others, and that they will inspire and stimulate. But above all it is hoped that they will encourage teachers to think constructively about their curricula and the needs of their pupils. It is not the intention of the research team to offer ready-made 'suggestions for teachers' suitable for immediate adoption. Such an intention would indeed defeat all that is envisaged. The concept of the developing pupil – experiencing, initiating, creating, and taking decisions – must be matched by the concept of the teacher who is effectively sharing these activities with him. The objective of this project is to assist more teachers and thereby more pupils to reach the take-off point for this partnership in education. Though material and information will be diffused throughout the Project – through publications, conferences, and discussion – the end-products will, it is hoped, be the diffusion of ideas and the stimulation of thinking. . . .[1]

All this, of course, presupposed that change might occur, so when discussing the impact of any agency it is important to identify what existed before and what is different now. Indeed, conjecture on what might have been, were it not for the intervention of a national project, may also be rewarding. It is admitted that change within design and craft has resulted from several quarters such as other Schools Council projects, teacher panels of examination boards and so on. In essence then, a partnership existed for much of the life of the project. Many factors may symbolize movement within education; it is sensible to assume that the establishment of a national project is itself a change; the provision of additional and different facilities within a school may be change; an increase in the number of pupils opting for courses may constitute change; so too may the adoption of different examination courses.

Beyond these, fundamental issues emerge if one is to judge the effective impact of the project. The character of the change process is paramount. Here lay the embryonic strength of the project inasmuch as its affairs were established and conducted as a reflection of need – a need that was identifiable and accepted by many teachers working in the field. Although the project was subsequently based in a University Department of Education it did not represent research and development in a separate or isolated way. The essence of activity – and this was another strength – lay in the mobilization and co-ordination of teachers in many parts of Britain.

It will be remembered that the Project commenced life as the *Research and Development Project in Handicraft*. It was not very long after that the more appropriate terminology *Design and Craft* was adopted. This reflected more accurately the nature of activity that the Project had begun to support. Since then there has been wide-spread adoption of this nomenclature; but it is more than semantics that concerns us here — though, in part, a new emphasis deserved a new title. This emphasis found two broad aspects emerging; one dealing with the expanding interpretation of 'design in education' and the other related to the developing requirement and confidence of teachers to act as 'curriculum planners'.

In dealing with the role of design in education it can be said that for many years educators appeared to be well-versed in the diverse nature of child development and the requirements within schools to meet the challenges of adult life. Those engaged in the teaching of 'practical' subject were often as aware of such factors as their colleagues immersed in the 'academic' disciplines. Despite this, it was clear that many programmes relying on the use of tools and materials fell short of broad accomplishment. All too often the making process predominated in an experience that should have also laid stress on the thinking process and the inherent social implications of a modern education.

If the influence of the Project is to be judged in terms of educational value, an indication may be seen in the balance of experience now expected of school pro-grammes. This balance conforms to the interpretation put forward by D.I.R. Porter H.M.I, in which he claims that courses should consist of

> education, of course; design, because we must prepare thoughtfully; technology, in the sense that it is for life and for living; and craft, because that is the means by which we achieve our purpose.[2]

In an endeavour to create a balance of such factors, it may appear that over-emphasis has been placed on the intellectual and social implications. Some quarters voiced hostile criticism at the apparent relegation of 'craft' aspects. Let it be stressed that in the designing and making process all elements are inter-dependent and that the action of fashioning materials at a work-bench cannot be superseded. It is, therefore, not necessary to debate the importance of craft skills; let us then discuss the nature of thinking skills which were inherently important in the project's philosophy.

The most valuable and useable long-term benefit of working with tools and materials stems from the individual's ability to think. This not only enhances the quality of one's own performance but may also be applied in order to come to grips with the needs of others and the ever increasing range of environmental problems. Thus the practice of thinking skills enables an individual to participate in decision-making and present the possibility of contributing to the development of the environment.

In order to bring elements of logical thinking into focus the project applied a flexible yet discernible design process. Constituent parts of this interrelate to cover all aspects of problem identification and solution. It is clear that if pupils are effectively to undertake problem-solving approaches they will be required to exercise abilities which enable them to enquire, communicate, analyse, synthesize, select, discriminate and evaluate. The Project was very much concerned with ways of allowing pupils to participate in these operations. The overall plan gained much credence and was successfully undertaken in a range of situations. Although space does not allow the full discussion of all aspects, value may be gained by highlighting the component of divergent thinking.

Until fairly recently work in school workshops was very much of a convergent nature. Pupils were frequently on the receiving end of decisions taken elsewhere and were often in receipt of a 'blue-print'. Sometimes these 'blue-prints' were intricately detailed and conveyed information relating to dimensions, type of constructional detail and procedural operations. With the advent of more outward-looking and open-ended teaching/learning situations, many pupils found themselves in what may be termed the 'blank paper' *fait accompli*. In many respects this was as disastrous as the 'blue-print' approach. It is not necessary to expound upon the likely input of pupils given a problem in a vacuum; the output of even gifted pupils requires teacher or resource based guidance. It was against this background that the design process emerged. Stress is placed on the necessity of recognizing and understanding the actual problem area; this is often a more difficult undertaking than the production of solutions. By debating ways in which problems may be presented by the teacher or identified by the pupils, we are in an area vastly different from the 'blue-print' mentioned earlier, where a third person had already identified the problem and suggested the solution.

Take also the idea of encouraging pupils to enquire in order to suggest a range of alternative solutions to a problem. We all know that in the past the 'blue-print' represented a single solution or at best pupils conjured a copy from a reputable book or converged on a single solution preconceived as a result of shop-window gazing or what had gone before in the particular workshop.

It will be seen that careful and detailed consideration of aspects of the design process gives rise to the possibility of engaging pupils in open-ended or divergent thinking patterns. For example, it may be worth questioning whether a coffee table — if this is the answer to a particular problem — really does need to consist of a wooden or wood substitute horizontal surface supported by four legs and a number of rails. It is not too difficult to get quite ordinary pupils to appreciate that a table may consist of anything but this form of construction; if this approach is taken it is evident that development may take place in a vastly enhanced range of materials and constructional techniques.

It is possible to duplicate open-endedness at almost all stages of a design process. The difficulty lies not so much in whether pupils are capable of active participation but to what degree or depth the activity is adopted. This will be conditioned by internal constraints of individual schools; today there is an awareness that in even the most 'traditional' arrangement some emphasis is required on aspects of the thinking process. The project's materials on this are daily assisting more teachers to incorporate this new dimension into their work.

Apart from work on the design process, equal emphasis was placed on the social implications of working with tools and materials. Several important growth points were identified. Of these two are selected for mention at this point.

One deals with the concept of community development. Here there is a clear intention to involve pupils in real problems in the outside community. These may be typified by the design and construction of play equipment for younger children, specialist equipment for handicapped people, the restoration of items of interest within the community, or the challenge of a practical problem allied to any outside body. As with so much work of the project there was inevitably a more important aspect than the production of hardware. For one thing, grappling with a social problem may lead to other even wider social issues. Take the instance of secondary school pupils undertaking an investigation of the needs of a nursery class attached to an infants' school. This revealed that although the school had made repeated requests to the LEA for funds with which to provide equipment, nothing had happened. Without being a social agitator, it is easy to see that young people are capable of asking not only themselves, but also others, why it was not possible to provide the resources and why a building would be provided without a range of necessary equipment. It will be seen that political implications may become inherent in such projects and before embarking on these it may be wise to realize this.

Another topic stems from the world of work. Here there is an attempt to help young people achieve an understanding of the basic factors that underlie work in say industry. By simulation in school workshops it is possible to come to grips with the role of foreman, production engineer, quality control inspector, store keeper and many others. Beyond this there is also the possibility of establishing activities in which market research, product design, advertising, packaging, selling, automation and unemployment are exploited. During the time of the Project a wealth of experience was established in this topic, and since then, the idea has grown to such an extent that many teachers are now familiar with the educational connotation of 'school-based factory days' as distinct from the apparent vocational interpretation.

The area where the Project's long lasting benefits may be seen relates to the management of these and other curriculum activities. No matter what nature innovation may take, a clear planning implication exists. Considerable stress was, therefore, placed on establishing a framework that could be demonstrated to be operational; to many this seemed to be in contrast to curriculum theories that at that time seemed remote from the day-to-day routine of school life. Thus a pattern emerged that served as a basis for all topics sponsored by the project.

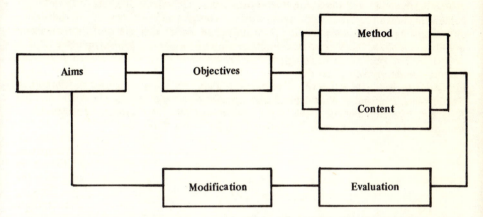

Diagram 1

Aims and objectives may be interpreted in as many ways as there are teachers. However, this should not prevent the presentation of clear, even clinical, statements of intent. The degree of precision and the grouping of aims and objectives will depend on the emphasis of a particular programme. Nevertheless, over a period of time a range of core objectives will be in evidence and with this in mind the project detailed these in terms of pupil behaviour. It was found that this had value in

1 helping to understand new programmes
2 providing a check-list to ensure adequate coverage of important objectives
3 aiding effective monitoring of progress
4 communicating to others the intentions of a project
5 bringing into focus the range of resources required for a particular assignment
6 helping pupils to come to grips with targets of a project
7 ensuring that realistic rather than over-ambitious intentions are adopted
8 establishing methods of assessment

The link between aims and objectives and evaluation became essential and teachers worked closely with the project in devising techniques of assessment appropriate for internal use and for the award of external examination certificates.

Finally, mention should be made of the way teachers came to appreciate the value of working as a team. This stemmed from reviewing *methods* by which goals may effectively be achieved. Teachers of art and craft were not alone in devising, operating and evaluating the Project's activities. Project work found teachers of home economics,

73

science, mathematics and humanities working side by side. In this way the Project demonstrated in the best way possible the positive aspects of integration. Since the breakthrough, developments have taken place that now find co-ordination within the curriculum commonplace.

These are some of the areas that have changed within the last few years; in many instances they represent tangible outcomes of the project. However, the true worth of the Project may yet lie in the 'hidden' influence and stimulation further to develop an important area of activity within our schools.

References
1 *Education Through the Use of Materials* Schools Council Working Paper 26, Evans Methuen (1969)
2 Porter D.I.R., HMI *Tailpiece, International Perspectives of Design Education*, Pemberton A.R. and Eggleston Professor S.J. Ed., University of Keele (1973)
Publications resulting from the Schools Council Design and Craft Project, published by Edward Arnold, London include: *Education through Design and Craft, Connections and Constructions, Looking at Design, Materials and Design — a fresh Approach, Design for Today, You Are a Designer, The Creative Use of Concrete, Design and Karting, Designing with Plastics.*
Filmstrips include: *Design in the Environment, Value for Money, Houses and Homes, Helping Out, Playthings, Kartways, Designing with Concrete, Joining Materials Together, Selection and use of Materials, Colour and Texture, Outline and Surfaces, Moulding and Casting, Materials and Tools, Shape, Form, Function.*

14
Damn design

G. PRESTON
Geoff Preston is Head of Design and Technical Studies at Wem, Salop. He spent fifteen years in industry and has completed a similar period teaching. Service with the Royal Air Force was with armaments and high explosives. His interests include model railways and fast electric model racing boats.

Abstract   Is obsession with the word 'design' a barrier to progress? This paper takes a serious look at the educational implications of the label. It gives a personal view of the limitations and the opportunities afforded by creative activities in a liberal education and has pertinent things to say about contemporary educational trends.

This paper has nothing to do with 617 squadron, or has it? Barnes Wallis was a designer. He took a simple geometric shape and from it produced a beautiful functional machine capable of being developed in one form or another for a considerable period of time. Then he changed to a different shape for a different purpose. We ought to be able to do exactly the same with the pupils in our schools. Our aim should involve the implanting of things beautiful, functional and fit for the purpose of *living*.

If I had to produce an analogy complementary to my philosophy of education, it would go something like this: think of the three axes of an isometric cube, each at 120 degrees to each other. Each axis represents a facet or concept of education:
1 literacy or the art of communication
2 numeracy or an understanding of the basic nature or aims of science
3 discovery or training in creative ability

For long enough we have thought that only these things matter. We forget at times the spirit of the individual. That which makes each one of us different from the other. But back to the isometric axes. A well balanced individual will endeavour to keep the three axes the same length. Often on the radio programme 'Desert Island Discs', in answer to Roy Plumley's question, 'Could you build [design] a shelter?', we hear the guests say that they are hopeless with their hands. What a sad reflection this is on those responsible for subject options. They too seem to have no creative ability.

If I enclose my isometric axes and produce a cube I see the spirit of man trying to burst out. If he succeeds in bursting out in one direction a genius is born. But for most of us it should be a matter of *expanding* in all directions. This is the job of education.

If the creative process is begun at the level of each individual, emotional involvement need not lead to confrontation, as often happens during adolescence. The beauty in design cannot be seen more clearly than when a person grasps some fundamental concept, and wishes to share the experience with others.

Design Ha! Ha!

I can honestly say that this idea was entirely evolved by the pupils without any help at all from the teacher. Such was the determination to try to justify the project – design – technology approach in the early days, that teachers made such a claim. It was as if their very status depended on being remote from the actual production process. How times have changed. All for the better. Now we find staff and pupils busily engaged in working together to produce almost anything, competing with British Leyland, or making aids for handicapped people. In the first instance they are no doubt driven on by the thought of a first prize material gain; in the second instance they are prepared to sacrifice much time and effort to help people less fortunate than themselves. Nevertheless both are contributing to the design process.

The multiplicity of organizations conceived during the past decade concerned with all aspects of curriculum development, each with its own abbreviated title, has almost exhausted the English alphabet. Some will die a natural death and the fittest will survive, so that cannot be a bad thing.

And what about aims and objectives? The thoughts which should be constantly pounding through our heads whenever we come into contact with our pupils. Here is a list for that essential part of education which no school should be without, (there exists a much better example in the Manchester area on covering an exercise book with wallpaper and Sellotape, but this is my contribution!):

School dinners, aims and objectives
The pupil on completing the course should be able to

1   tell the difference between gravy, sauce and custard
2   consume sufficient for his energy requirements without stopping for breath or spilling a quantity down the back of sir's neck
3   distinguish the shape of a knife, fork and spoon, and return them to the correct receptacle on leaving
4   consume spaghetti in an orderly manner.

Even the awkward squad manage item 4 with some dexterity. They can also work out the goal average of their favourite soccer team with some accuracy even when they have no real interest in mathematics. The point I am trying to make is that we should allow ourselves to participate in some activities for the sheer pleasure of it, rather than try to evaluate every move.

Let the pupil out of the box

Are we moving fast enough? Let us take a quick look back and a long look forward. Ten years ago I spent a year at Loughborough. Two Schools Council Projects were at that time gestating, one at Loughborough and the other at Keele. Ten years later, despite tremendous efforts, only now is the material being published. Yet, in the United States each area has its own team producing material for a Curriculum Services Division. They are considerably free from petty restrictions and are closely involved with teaching and feedback. The best we can offer are a few dedicated Teacher/Advisers supported by even fewer LEAs. Much of their work is concerned with re-staffing schools in their areas, giving them insufficient time for original thinking.

A recent television programme for the Open University course PET 271, 'Technology for Teachers', showed what is being achieved at Mons in Belgium. At the *Ecole Normale* (Teacher Education), technological literacy is being approached in an enlightened way. In-service courses are being attended by both men and women teachers of all disciplines.

Within the Teacher Education College there is a school (*Ecole d'application*) which is used for teaching practice. The feedback is immediate. At last someone has associated teacher training with education in schools.

Art Garfunkel, talking recently on the radio, said that 'much of the development of an [record] album evolves almost by accident. Something is tried in several different ways and all of a sudden it clicks'. Surely this is design at a high level. What he did not make so clear was the fact that much hard work with basic concepts was there already, put there by careful thought and wise tuition. 'Accidents' of this type only happen after painstaking research. Geodetics are only triangles but it is the use they are put to that really matters.

Comprehensive education has encouraged more pupils each year to opt for courses in which they are interested, rather than those which used to be demanded by the universities and other higher educational establishments. Consequently if these higher spheres of education wish to fill their courses they will have to take a broader view of future applicants' qualifications. Students are at present taking A levels in the following mixture: Mathematics – giving a foot in the sciences; History – giving a foot in the arts; Geography – because they like it. Education has witnessed such dramatic changes during the past thirty years. Dare I suggest that by the year 2000 specialist subject teachers will have disappeared completely.

Japanese youngsters are not as creative as the older generations would like. This feeling was reported recently. Perhaps their education, like ours, has stifled children into fixed patterns of adult thought.

Did the breaching of the three dams in Germany at the end of World War Two do any good? Did it make any contribution to the successful conclusion of the conflict? Are we who are supporting design – control – technology making any useful contribution to education? The Lancaster crews had the courage to use the bomb and drop it. Many teachers have had the courage and belief to use the design approach.

As the Industrial Revolution gathered momentum the nailmakers of the Midlands had no alternative but to diversify or die. Previously, civilizations along the River Nile failed to diversify and they did perish. Thousands of people stood outside the British Museum several years ago, prepared to wait half a day to see for half an hour the wonderful treasures of Tutankhamun. What design, what craftsmanship, and yet their civilization was unable to survive. What did they neglect?

Getting into shape

Here is a short starter course for teachers to use. It is suitable for most abilities and can be made more difficult in order to extend the quicker pupils, given a little care and thought. It is intended to precede the Control Technology Structures Course, and is designed for boys and girls of mixed ability in the second or third year at a secondary school.

Aim: to obtain enjoyment in developing methods for solving problems
Objectives: to develop the ability to test ideas
to discover alternative ways of placing shapes together to form patterns
to develop a co-ordination between hand and eye using templets
to associate a popular sport fixture-list with a mathematical concept
to show ability to visualize shapes from different positions in two dimensions

The course consists of five topics: Tessellations 1, Tessellations 2 (in which Tessellations 1 is given a third dimension), Fun and Imagination Shapes, Random Free Abstracts, and Symmetry. The complete course is relational in its structure, although each individual part is simple linear in its format. The degree of structure is tight because each individual step is small and the follow-up sheet provided enables the pupil to progress with plenty of sign-posts and to check whether he is right or wrong. The structure is intended to teach some facts, but mainly relationships.

Pupils are given a sheet explaining what the aims and objectives are before they start. Patterns, worksheets and wall charts give a variety of teaching display. The assignment sheet and follow-up sheet for Tessellations 1 is given below.

TESSELLATIONS 1
The basic shapes are a triangle, diamond, hexagonal, square, rectangle, and a square squared. (*see figure 1*)
The length of the sides of the triangle should be 20 mm, and the sides of all the shapes should be equal, or in a ratio of 2:1. Templates are required to make one of each shape, then pairs of shapes can be drawn around to see how they fit together in different ways. More elaborate designs can be developed using geometrical shapes (triangles with hexagons, squares with diamonds, or any other combination), and imagination shapes (animals, fishes, caricatures, vehicles, space vehicles). The key words in this assignment are equilateral, isosceles, scalene, dot, line, area, symmetry and atomic structures.

Assignment sheet
1 Take one of each different shape.
2 Using the triangles as a basic shape
   (i) how many triangles are there in the diamond?
   (ii) how many triangles are there in the hexagon?
   (iii) can you give another geometrical name for the diamond?
3 Using the small square as a basic shape
   (i) how many small squares are there in the rectangle?
   (ii) how many small squares are there in the large square?
   (iii) how many rectangles are there in the large square?
4 In your project design book draw around each shape with a pencil and give each shape a number as shown in fig. 1 above.
5 (i) Measure the length of the sides of shapes 1, 2, 3 and 4 in fig. 1. What do you notice?
   (ii) Measure the length of the sides of shapes 5 and 6 in fig. 1. What do you notice?
6 You will be able to fit the shapes together in pairs (see fig. 2).
7 See how many different ways you can fit each pair together. There are at least two ways in which the diamond and the triangle can be fitted together. But note that fig. 2(b) is the same as fig. 2(a) only upside down, and should not be counted as a different way.

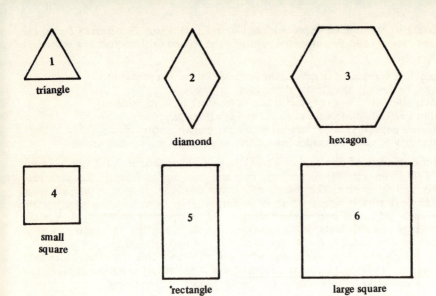

triangle

diamond

hexagon

small square

'rectangle

large square

Figure 1

Figure 2

8 When you pair the shapes together
  (i) draw around them in your book
  (ii) draw a separate diagram for each different pairing.
9 It will help you to check if you imagine that each shape is a football team and draw up a fixture list:
  1 v 2
  1 v 3   2 v 3
  1 v 4   etc.
  1 v 5
  1 v 6
10 How many pairings or fixtures will be needed if the six shapes are to 'play' each other once only?
11 Each time you find a different way of joining or pairing the sides of the shapes together, put a tick by the appropriate 'fixture', eg 4 v 5√.
12 Which pair of shapes fit together differently most times?
Follow-up sheet
  2 See fig. 3
    (i) there are two triangles in the diamond
    (ii) there are six triangles in the hexagon
    (iii) the diamond could be called a *rhombus*.

78

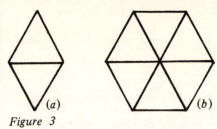

Figure 3

3 See fig. 4
  (i) there are two small squares in the rectangle
  (ii) there are four small squares in the large square
  (iii) there are two rectangles in the large square.

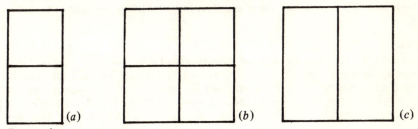

Figure 4

5 (i) they are all the same length
  (ii) they are twice as long as 5(i), or the ends of the rectangle are the same length.
7 There are at least thirty-nine different ways. See fig. 5 for just a few.

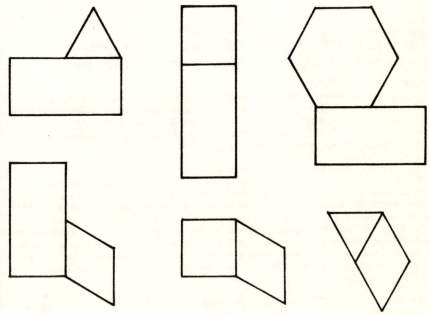

Figure 5

9 Fixture list:

  1 v 2
  1 v 3   2 v 3
  1 v 4   2 v 4   3 v 4
  1 v 5   2 v 5   3 v 5   4 v 5
  1 v 6   2 v 6   3 v 6   4 v 6   5 v 6

10 There are fifteen pairings or fixtures if the shapes are to play each other or fit against each other once only.

12 Six times seems to be the maximum number that shapes 5 and 2 will fit together, but perhaps there are more.

EVALUATION

With the use of follow-up sheets giving answers regularly it is fairly easy to assess how far and at what speed a pupil is progressing. It is also easy to check where parts of the course have been misunderstood. These can then be rewritten in the light of evidence acquired.

Conclusion

State education has relied on the ideas of voluntary workers in the sunday schools and youth organizations for many years, in order to motivate the uninterested. The danger is that we have ruined the former and mis-used the latter. There is an urgent need for teachers of vision to initiate the teaching of progressive methods to fulfil a need. In fact to survive as a nation, or civilization for that matter, we must continue whatever the cost.

In true design the best idea is usually chosen from a number of alternatives. We have no alternative. As Professor Laithwaite remarked in issue 9 of the S.C.S.S.T. news, 'Let's change, if only for the hell of it'. So damn design if you dare.

15

The role of the designer within a multi-disciplinary organization with observations on design education

JOHN RAWSTHORNE

John Rawsthorne works for Northampton Development Corporation and is in charge of print design in a group directly responsible to the Development Corporation's General Manager for publicising the opportunities offered by Northampton. He received his Dip TD from Liverpool College of Art in 1968 and worked as typographic designer in a printer's studio for two years before going to Northampton in 1970.

Abstract   The paper looks at the role of the 'print' designer within an organization which embraces a wide range of activities at both national and local levels. It illustrates the prime considerations of selling an idea as opposed to a product; looks at 'design' education from an employer's point of view, and also the reasons why management employ designers, how those reasons can affect the 'design' process and consequently the final product. It proves the value, in design education, of splitting course time into a definite 'time to product' and 'experimental research' structure. It questions the value of an education system which promotes a system of the qualified student becoming a teacher without having the broader base of commercial experience, thus teaching what he has been taught. Finally, there is comment on the individual benefits which the design student attains even if he never practises professionally.

The town of Northampton, where the 1976 Institute of Craft Education Conference is taking place, is an historic town that is currently being expanded.

The primary object of the expansion is to provide homes for people from the

Greater London area who are in real housing need and the town is to grow to 230,000 people by the mid 1980s. The organization set up to carry this expansion into effect is Northampton Development Corporation, which has the task of providing the new houses, arranging that all the shops, schools and social facilities are made available and ensuring that there are jobs for the people who move to Northampton.

The Development Corporation therefore has to attract new industry and workers to the town, which it aims to do by publicizing the opportunities that Northampton has to offer; and at the same time it has a responsibility to keep the existing population, some 130,000 of them, informed of what is going on in their town.

At the outset, the decision was taken that the Development Corporation's public relations activities would be carried out by people employed in the organization and answering directly to the General Manager. A team has gradually been built up which has, since its very early days, included typographic designers. Why does an organization like this employ its own designers? The argument could be put forward that an advertising agency could provide the same service. There is little doubt that many agencies have expertise that is second to none in selling tangible products like soap, beer or cigarettes. But what Northampton has to sell is an idea; people who are considering a move must immediately think of Northampton as the most suitable location for their organization or for themselves as individuals, and it is to this end that Northampton Development Corporation's publicity is directed. The inevitably long chain of communication between the client and the agency might well lead to errors in interpretation, and make it difficult to reflect the changes in emphasis that are needed because of external factors. The agency, by virtue of having many clients, would find greater difficulty in identifying with Northampton's interests and objectives than does a designer working in the organization and having direct contact with the management. Furthermore, by controlling its own publicity, management can ensure that the budget is used to the best advantage; it can see what is being produced at any stage of production, and can, if necessary, make amendments without incurring too much wasted expenditure. Publicity budgets can be made to realize their full worth rather than disappearing into agency overheads!

As a new organization, the Development Corporation had to project itself through every means available, but the starting point was the basic requirement of stationery, or rather the creation of a house style at a time when no one really knew how broad would be the area of work to which it would be applied. The house style was laid down initially to cover stationary requirements and has subsequently been modified to incorporate information signing and site signboards. Basically the house style was kept to a simple word form and the typeface chosen was Univers designed by Adrian Frutiger. The reasons for the choice of face were its availability in metal, film and instant lettering systems, and its visual impact in a wide variety of uses. The other element in house style was the use of a colour with two greens being the final choice, a light lime green for external signs and a darker, more subdued colour for the stationery.

Having arrived at a basic style the second phase was the process of selling Northampton by establishing an identity through design. Advertising was the next area to which the house style was applied, making use of the logotype and identifying Northampton Development Corporation with Northampton. The range of work increased, calling for different applications of style, and modifications became necessary as new requirements arose. This meant that both the designer and the house style have had to remain flexible. The range of work now covered includes advertising, brochures, exhibitions, forms and anything else which comes along. The smallest piece of designed print is for a matchbox and probably the largest is for 16-sheet poster advertising.

The whole range of print is aimed at selling Northampton and the prime motivation comes from management, which has an awareness of its customers and a sensitivity to their needs. It has been a policy decision that Northampton Development Corporation has so far concentrated more on the attraction of firms than on the attraction of individuals. Hence most advertising is aimed at companies, informing them of the broad advantages Northampton can offer. When management has made its policy decision, the implementation is expected to show quickly and effectively. It is here that the management's approach to design bears direct relevance to the 'print' designer's success or failure to communicate effectively. If the management gives an inflexible brief in terms of content and design, the designer is reduced to a mere mechanic. If there is no brief, the designer has no direction to follow and the results achieved can be a waste of time and effort. Therefore the first ingredient for the designer is a brief, outlining the broad structure required, identifying the points requiring emphasis and yet leaving sufficient flexibility for the designer to bring his design training and experience to bear on solving the problems inherent in any design. Designers are employed to express the management's policy in printed form. It is therefore up to the designer as an individual to build up a relationship of mutual understanding and respect with the management. This may take time, but the establishment of such a relationship can be as important to the end product as the designer's ability to design.

It may be interesting to mention that Northampton Development Corporation has always applied the rule that neither the copy nor the design is sacrosanct. If the designer thinks the copy does not express the idea clearly enough, there is the opportunity to discuss with the copywriter different ways of expressing the idea. There must therefore be the opportunity for the copywriter to comment on the design. This kind of situation helps to create an atmosphere where people with different skills can contribute to the final product. Unfortunately, because of outside pressures, copy dates, deadlines etc, there are occasions when this kind of exchange of ideas is impracticable. Both copywriter and designer simply do the best they can in the time they have available. Whatever solution is arrived at, the final decision of approval or rejection of the design, rests with the management. If the design is rejected, then the designer must re-think the job; he must bear in mind the reasons for failure of the first design, and achieve a solution acceptable to all concerned. This kind of situation can be invaluable to the designer, because it creates a certain kind of pressure which presents a personal challenge to him as an individual. It is the sort of situation which is quite common on a commercial design level, where the designer is serving a number of clients.

Most of the people involved in business management are unlikely to have any formal design education experience, and so there is likely to be a wide gap between the designer's thinking and the management's appreciation of that thinking. It is here that the designer must learn new techniques and understanding. If the designer has done his job properly and presented his rough designs for approval, he approaches what could be called the moment of truth. Even if the design problems have been solved to the designer's satisfaction there is the chance that management can say they do not like the result. It is here that personal appreciation comes into effect and it is in this area that the designer must learn to sell his product. In the design environment of college, it is the lecturer who must act as client, but he has the advantage of being able to talk in design terms; the language is common to both student and lecturer. But outside the college environment, the client is less likely to be able to communicate his reactions, and the designer must work out what his client means when he says the result is not quite what had been expected. Perhaps students would benefit if lecturers could sometimes forget their design language and understanding, thus stimulating the circumstances likely to be encountered in a work situation.

The designer will meet prejudice of many kinds when he starts to practise professionally, and whilst it would be impossible to simulate every kind of prejudice likely to be experienced, lecturers with commercial experience should be able to bring that experience into play within the educational environment. If one of the purposes of design education is to produce designers capable of producing commercially acceptable products, more work should be done to acquaint students with a situation as close to that as will be found outside the college.

Basically the management employs its own designers to produce designs and buy print, making sure that its money works effectively. The designer finds himself designing, producing artwork, negotiating with printers, reproduction houses, typesetters, artists, photographers and organizing any other service required for the final product. In the end he finds that a fraction of his time is spent on design, the remainder being spent on the organization and mechanics which go into producing print. No college can be expected to teach everything to the student and when the student eventually starts work and can begin to apply what he has been taught he must understand that he has a lot to learn about business. He is no longer designing for other designers but for the people who employ him: he may find that designs which would call forth praise from other designers may be unacceptable in the work situation.

In design education, course time can be split into specific areas of study. Graphics, illustration and typography deal with particular design subjects whilst print technology relates to all three. It is of the utmost importance that students are made aware of what can and cannot be achieved when it comes to reproducing, in print, their original ideas. What looks superb in rough form may be completely impractical when it comes down to mass production. An understanding of print limitations is essential to anyone hoping to work as a 'print' designer. I am not saying that a designer must be able to run a four-colour press but he should be aware of the limitations that the graphic reproduction processes impose on his designs. If any doubt exists in the designer's mind as to whether his design can be accomplished he should consult his printer or reproduction house before the job gets to the point of finished artwork. Printers, because of their experience can often help the designer to solve problems before they arise, at, say, the platemaking stage. Such problems can be very expensive to correct, and the 'print' designer's job is to design within certain cost limitations.

If print and design departments could be persuaded to plan their courses in conjunction with one another, work produced by the design departments could provide course work for trade print students. This should help both the design and the print students to achieve a better understanding of each other's problems. It would also give practical experience to design students before they became employed, which would be of immense practical value to them in their subsequent contacts with printers.

Another aspect of design education which could afford help to students when they start work would be the imposition of definite time limitations on some of their design projects. If a designer has one week to produce a result, there is no point in making excuses for failure to produce the design; a design is required. Perhaps more time would enable the designer to produce a better result, but in practice there are time limits which have to be met. Within such projects the student would note the area of work which he would have developed had more time been available. These notes could then provide a basis for experimental research and the results could be related to the original project. This would enable both the student and the lecturer to assess development of ideas whilst providing research work with a real foundation.

I have already mentioned the importance of making students aware of the problems to be faced when working as designers. Obviously lecturers without commercial experience of some description would find difficulty in presenting these problems to students in a realistic way. As I believe this aspect of training to be exceedingly important, I must question the present system whereby students who have recently qualified go straight on to ATD courses. Art as an experience is without doubt of benefit but surely if this is the major source of educational supply, the situation must arise where teachers can teach only what they themselves have been taught. There can be little opportunity for the development of new techniques and greater understanding of the ever changing problems in design. Perhaps the system might be improved if prospective teachers were barred from ATD until they had spent some time broadening their experience and making themselves aware of problems other than education. Student teachers would then be better equipped to relate their education problems to the real situations which they know from personal experience are to be found outside.

Design education makes the student visually aware of objects around him, appreciative of subtle changes of colour and, in short, provides him with a basic understanding of all that can be called art. The student has the choice of whether he develops that understanding or allows it just to become part of his overall experience. If the design student chooses not to practice professionally when he finishes his course, the fact that he has been made aware of design stands him in good stead, no matter what job he ends up doing. In understanding the process of design the student gains a thinking process which can be applied to many different types of problems. This in itself makes the study of design useful to .society in the long term, and must eventually improve the general standards of design and design appreciation.

16
In-service teacher training/education in design/technology in schools
D.M. SHAW

David Shaw is Senior Lecturer at the Education Unit, Lanchester Polytechnic, Rugby. He is moderator/assessor in Design and Technology for CSE/CEE. Mr. Shaw writes and lectures widely on design education and gave the Institute of Craft Education 1972 Avery Hill Conference lecture on 'Plastics as Educational Media'.

Abstract   This contribution identifies the role of technology and design in contemporary education. It differentiates between personal and professional requirements and suggests ways in which needs may be met through guidance and problem-solving activities.

While, during recent years much has been said, written, and, in some cases, done about introducing and developing the concepts and practice of design and technology education in schools, very little action has been taken adequately to equip serving teachers either personally or professionally to deal with this now potentially wide-reaching area of the curriculum.

There are many who would suggest that the grass roots movement towards an interdisciplinary and occasionally multimedia approach does not really call for a reappraisal or review of the teacher's role. He will continue to 'do his own thing in his own way in any case.' Such an ostrich-like attitude ignores not only the body of information and knowledge presently available both pragmatic and philosophical in origin but also some of the findings of the Royal College of Art Research Project in Design in general education which will be made available early in 1976.

Elsewhere, Mr G White describes initial teacher training education in the field of design education. The purpose of this article is to attempt to identify the needs of teachers serving in this field and then to outline some of the ways in which their needs are being – or should be – met.

Though design and technology in education can embrace activities covering a very wide spectrum of the curriculum, in the context of this discussion the teachers concerned will be those generally involved in the potentially related areas of art, craft, home economics and applied science and technology. Historically it would be largely true to say that few teachers have in the past received initial training and education appropriate to fulfilling their needs in teaching this extended range of activities. In practice and in general, their training was either art based, craft/home-economics biased or traditional science for the secondary teachers most likely to be involved, and generally class orientated for teachers in the primary field.

Colleges and departments of education are now beginning to turn their attention to the production of teachers with a broad design and technology-based background, but the fact remains that the majority of teachers have received little or no reorientation training/education – to use the DES 'INSET' phraseology – which will better prepare them for their wider reaching role in design and technology education.

The foundations of design education, ranging across an introduction to appropriate aspects of technology, logical approaches to problem solving ('the problem – solution interactive couple' as Professor Archer describes it) two and three dimensional realization and design, the intuitive expression of the self and visual expression and communication, should be laid down in the primary or middle years of schooling. Recent national research shows that few primary and middle schools provide such educational experience on any realistic scale. *Curriculum differences for Boys and Girls* DES educational survey No. 21 HMSO 975 also makes it very clear that the attitudes which engender separate three-dimensional experiences for boys and girls are to no-one's advantage and that girls are particularly disadvantaged by this situation which progresses in various forms right up through the secondary stage.

Good teachers are invariably busy teachers but reorientation of some attitudes and the extension of the width of their experience and expertise is necessary if design and technology is to develop in schools as it ought. The School Technology Forum, the teachers' arm of the SCSST, has recently put forward detailed proposals for a pilot, in-service education course 'Technology in the Middle Years' to provide an opportunity for technology to be seen and appreciated as an enrichment of the curriculum as a whole rather than as a narrow subject or speciality. This course will be run at the Education Unit, Lanchester Polytechnic, Rugby during the Summer Term of 1976.

Many teachers, particularly primary-trained class teachers, lacking science qualifications are frightened by the very name. This stems from a total misconception of what technology, as it applies to pupils of this age range, is really about. Parallel to this is the other major misconception that design is in some mystical manner connected only with art. 'I could never draw and therefore this design education business is not for me!' Back to the knitting and the teapot stand!

Such blinkered views, while understandable, must be generally replaced by a wider comprehension by teachers of what design and technology in schools is all about if these complementary areas of study are to become universally recognized and entered into.

Such is the situation at primary level and it is not much better in the middle schools where staff are in the main ex-primary trained class teachers or secondary trained specialists. Yet this is the educational field where the seeds of design and technology education must be sown; when children's fundamental attitudes are developed and their interests most easily aroused as has been shown by 'Science 5-13' and 'Art & Craft Education 8-13' – both Schools' Council Projects.

In secondary schools, despite the findings and the availability of teaching material from 'Project Technology' and 'Craft and Design' projects, the fact remains that in these subject areas where development could and should take place, too often we find greater stress placed on the reasons why progress cannot be made rather than on those why it should be. It is all too easy to blame the teacher for not attempting to take up the challenge, but commenting as a teacher of long standing, I feel that the problems are such that sympathy and assistance, rather than criticism, are called for.

Leaving aside the perennial problems of inadequate facilities, insufficient financial resources and so on, which will always remain, where else lie the main problems and difficulties, the disincentives which need to be removed, so that forward movement in this area of curriculum development with a sense of purpose and a real hope of success can be achieved? A number of questions spring readily to mind

1 What is necessary to bring about the adequate provision of serving teachers who will possess appropriate expertise and experience?
2 How can the attitudes of head teachers and others be so changed that design and technology are encouraged to take their reasonable and rightful place in the curriculum and in the timetable?
3 What exactly are the constraints within which such development can take place, and how in the present economic climate can positive steps be taken to help the teacher overcome them?
4 What are the specific needs and requirements of teachers? How can in-service training and education be used most effectively to fulfil those requirements?
  How far are these needs common to all those engaged in this field of education and how far are they particularized or individual?

Individual teachers will have their own views and possibly answers on these questions. Here I am concerned with expressing a personal viewpoint on a few of the problems arising from question 4 above.

Where design and technology education in schools has either been inadequately initiated or has not realized its potential level of effectiveness, personal research suggests that the reason for this partial failure lies not with the pupils or the principles or concepts of design and technology education but with a lack of appropriate training for the teachers concerned. Hence the real need for in-service training and education to enable the teacher to clear these twin hurdles of lack of specific professional training and experience in using appropriate approaches in design and technology to their fullest educational potential. Generally the teachers' in-service training and educational needs will fall into two main categories.

1 Professional needs

These are associated with the production of appropriate and sensible course objectives and the means of implementing them, and the organization and administration of design and technology based studies using systems and methods appropriate to the type of school in which he serves. This aspect of the teacher's need has generally been neglected both in initial training and in the provision of appropriate and realistic in-service courses. Few teachers ever receive positive guidance on the evaluation of their work and the assessment or appraisal of the attainment or progress of their pupils. Yet if assessment is to be valid it must be directly related to specific and measurable course objectives. Too often, even at the level of external examinations, performance in design and technology and associated studies is subjected to loose and vague approaches in its evaluation which are largely lacking in objectivity. Systematic course planning and its implementation does not happen by chance, yet all too few teachers have received professional guidance in appropriate management techniques, which in industry and commerce are commonplace.

Timetabling is not a form of Headmaster's crossword puzzle as some cynics might suppose. Balancing curricular requirements against available facilities, staff, pupils and the clock is a management problem of considerable magnitude. Head teachers simply cannot be expected to inject new topics or interdisciplinary modes of study into existing timetabling patterns unless the staff concerned can justify and detail for him requirements which can be seen to be educationally sound and practicable.

Many secondary schools have adopted the block timetable as a means of allowing design and technology departments in the lower forms to develop their own inter-disciplinary approaches. But this in itself solves no problems at all! In fact it presents the teacher with more problems which will require organizational and administrational as well as educational answers.

While no one pattern of pupil experience can ever be universally appropriate, a major requirement of in-service training is that it must provide teachers with the opportunity to identify possible approaches and ways of approaching the whole business of teaching in this area of the curriculum.

Some school courses comprising work in design and technology will be on a subject basis; others will be concerned with the overlay or enrichment of other of the curriculum as a whole. The nature and approach to studies and activities for pupils of different ages and abilities calls for a considerable degree of professional awareness and expertise for which many teachers are presently seeking guidance. Secondary specialists are too often unaware of the tremendous strides which have been made in teaching methods in the primary field and which are particularly appropriate for design and technology activities for the older pupils. Team teaching projects and assignments, the availability and use of appropriate teaching materials and opportunities to try them out, to devise and discuss experimental approaches with like-minded colleagues of similar and dissimilar backgrounds — all these should form a part of the professional aspect of in-service courses for teachers involved in design and technology education in schools.

2 Personal needs

The personal needs of the teacher are wide ranging but among them will be the provision of facilities to enable the teacher to extend his personal knowledge, experience and expertise in design, technology and its realization in two and three dimensional aspects across a range of media and to relate such work to the needs of society. Too often such work is restricted because the teacher feels inadequate. A joint learning situation where teacher and pupil seek for answers together, both gaining new knowledge and experience is probably the most fruitful of all. Too frequently however secondary teachers are over-specialized as a result of their training and prior experience and find great difficulty even in communicating meaningfully with each other, yet alone working closely and effectively with colleagues across the disciplines involved in the design/technology spectrum of education.

Design and technology in education must not be conceived in a narrow sense or practiced within a restricted framework. The complex relationships between design, technology and society call for a wider view than that which has been previously provided in initial teacher education courses, and thus teachers from all contributing disciplines and backgrounds need opportunities to extend their own horizons. Such extensions should include sampling work in other areas of the study outside the teachers' immediate experience to develop greater understanding of the objectives and contributions of others to their own discipline, and an awareness of the contribution and cross fertilization which the teacher can make through the free availability of his own expertise to others.

The changing pattern of education in the middle years has brought about a massive increase in the number of middle schools over the past few years, and has increased the opportunities for primary and secondary teachers to bridge the gap which has so often separated them. The success or failure of these new schools will depend to a considerable extent on the willingness of staff to adapt to the ethos of the middle school which is neither wholly primary (child centred) nor traditional secondary (subject centred).

As previously stated, given positive guidance during in-service education and training these teachers will have an increasing contribution to make to design and technology education for all children.

Many secondary teachers, rightly anxious to run appropriate courses leading to external examinations, feel the need for guidance and here again in-service training and education courses have an important role. Through discussion and guided practical involvement, teachers will develop greater awareness of the potential of their own courses and greater confidence in their ability to plan and organize them and utilize effective systems of evaluation.

But the opportunities for in-service training and education must be provided. As was suggested at the RCA Summer School in Design in General Education (July 1975) in-service teacher training and education should not be perceived as an optional extra but a component of the career structure of every teacher.

In a rapidly changing world, where most of our pupils are likely to change the direction of their career two or three times during their working life, teachers cannot be expected to serve the changing needs of an ever-changing society without adequate opportunity to re-appraise their work, to take a fresh look at their role as educationalists and to re-vitalize their teaching. The DES 'INSET' document offers positive guidelines in this direction but it requires wide implementation if it is to have any real and lasting effect.

The overall pattern of appropriate in-service training and education may involve courses of both long and short duration, of generalized and specialized study run locally and at educational institutions which can provide appropriate facilities and expertise. LEA advisory staff have a vital role to play and excellent though all too often limited work is being carried out at local levels where short and part-time courses are linked to classroom development and trials.

At present however there are very few opportunities for teachers to attend in-service training/education courses which meet the two major requirements, professional and personal, outlined above.

Courses Provided

Specialist short courses in certain aspects of Schools Technology are run at the National Centre for Schools Technology and Summer Schools arranged by the Institute of Craft Education and the DES and SATROS provide a useful additional service.

At the Education Unit of Lanchester Polytechnic where in-service courses in technology and design education have been pioneered over the last eight years, four day residential courses are currently being offered. It is hoped that more advanced courses of longer duration will be mounted when the national pattern of teacher training and education, presently in a state of flux, has been clarified.

Other educational establishments offer courses on an *ad hoc* basis but the present savage cuts in LEA educational budgets have in many cases resulted in a severe cutback in in-service facilities and the availability of financial support for teachers to attend external courses. Just how long design and technology education in schools can feed off its own fat — (and there's little enough of that!) — is open to doubt. One fact is certain, teachers need and are calling for help in the form of in-service training and education, but if the principles and practice of design and technology in schools are not to die of starvation or strangulation, then widespread in-service education is called for.

Throughout this paper, I have linked design and technology. Some might argue the supremacy of one or the other, but design and technology in schools are so closely linked in terms of potential educational experience and methodology that to try to differentiate or discriminate too closely is a somewhat pointless and rather academic pursuit. What they share in common is much more important than the areas in which they may occasionally appear to differ. Indeed the S.T.F, on page 6 of S.T.F Working Paper No. 1, February 1974, stated 'The problem-solving activity of design is the heart of the technological process.'

17

Equipping for schools technology

G.H. STARMER

Geoffrey H. Starmer is Senior Adviser for Further and Higher Education with a responsibility for Schools Technology, Northamptonshire LEA, and was previously Head of the Education Unit of Lanchester Polytechnic. He is author of two units for the Open University course 'Technology for Teachers' and two handbooks on industrial archaeology for Schools Council Project Technology.

Abstract   Taking the definition of technology as the purposeful application of knowledge and techniques, this paper amplifies the view that the eventual stage of any schools technology should be the solution, normally in hardware form, of problems related to real needs. It details items required, outlines types, features and uses of materials and equipment and gives clues to sources.

Introduction

The stages in a typical approach to satisfy the needs of the stated definition are shown in diagrammatic form in fig. 1. From this, it follows that as a result of participating in schools technology activities our pupils should be able to

(a)   Analyze a need so as to identify the real problem
(b)   Obtain and select information appropriate to the solution of a particular problem
(c)   Suggest several different solutions for a given problem
(d)   Make considered judgments in selecting the optimum solution
(e)   Communicate ideas and their practical implication, to others
(f)   Choose appropriate systems, components and materials for the implementation of the optimum solution
(g)   Use appropriate methods of production and assembly to produce the hardware solution
(h)   Evaluate whether the hardware solution does satisfy the originally specified need
(i)   Analyze faults and deficiencies so as to propose and implement modifications to the hardware solution.

These learning outcomes are valid for all pupils provided that the initial 'needs' in the problems presented to them allow solutions that can be achieved by a standard of each learning outcome appropriate to the pupils' ability levels. To be able to achieve these learning outcomes there are a number of prerequisites expected of the pupil, such as the following

1 Skills in manipulating a wide range of materials
2 Appreciation of the different properties of a wide range of materials and their applications
3 Familiarity with assembly techniques for several types of system
4 Knowledge of a range of scientific principles and concepts
5 Ability to communicate orally, in writing or visually
6 Experience of working with simple structures, energy sources, transmissions and control methods to satisfy given conditions
7 Appreciation of use of different measuring techniques under practical as well as laboratory conditions.

The traditional areas of the curriculum cover a number of these including knowledge of scientific principles and concepts and skills in manipulating materials. However this latter implies a wide range of materials and the manipulation of plastics is considered as part of that activity as is the equipment required. This aspect is not discussed here.

On the other hand, some of the prerequisites listed are not catered for in this way and are often parts of courses called technology; presumably because this title seems to present a modern image better than the more appropriate term 'technical studies'. These 'preparation for technology' courses also require equipment that might not otherwise be available in the school and it is anticipated that some of the equipment considered later in this paper will also meet many of these requirements.

Hardware

Consideration of a number of school projects[1] shows that the needs for equipment could be grouped under the following headings:
    Structures
    Energy Sources
    Transmissions
    Control
    Measurement
Some of the equipment under these headings might already be available in other parts of the school and we must check to see that each extra item of equipment is justified, possibly on the basis of likely frequency and duration of use.

Structures

In all hardware solutions, there will be a requirement to hold the component parts in correct relationship. Structure is used here to cover the means of satisfying this particular requirement. In many cases this has been achieved simply by clamping the parts to a stout bench by G-cramps and these can be needed so often that it is inadvisable to rely on their availability from the woodwork room.

If the hardware is to be movable it will need to have a self-contained structure and often this will be of wood and/or metal, making considerable use of skills and techniques for manipulating these materials. However, in many instances it is possible to utilize reusable components such as Meccano or Hybridex (available through the National Centre for Schools Technology). For larger structures, Dexion or Handi-angle can also provide reusable components. If a supply of tubular fittings are available, appropriate tubing can be utilized but there can be difficulties in providing easy mounting for any items that have to be attached to the resulting structure. There is a number of plastic constructional systems available but these are often of doubtful value in achieving the desired learning outcomes from schools technology in that they require techniques of assembly which are not applicable to other types of structure.

For mounting items which are intrinsically circular in section, a range of Terry clips has proved worthwhile, whilst for circular objects such as lenses, plastic drain pipes and fittings, specially formed rings have been used to good effect by T.G. Jones of the Education Unit, Lanchester Polytechnic.

In the preliminary stages of evaluation, laboratory clamp stand systems provide quickly assembled and altered structures, even if not very elegantly. Some structures need to be mobile and both the Dexion and Handi-angle ranges include castors of different sizes but there are frequent requirements for larger wheels. Bicycle wheels provide a ready-made solution when light, circular structures are needed.

So far, structures have been considered in the context of holding together solid parts of a system but there is often a need to hold or contain fluids or loose material: plastic buckets and oil drums can meet this need. It is useful to collect a whole range of sizes of container.

Energy Sources

There are many different requirements for energy ranging from those for straightforward mechanical energy output to occasions when a heat or a light source is needed. For mechanical output, electric motors have been a common choice. The very small varieties have been acquired from discarded toys. For both these and the larger motors sold for model purposes, it is essential that their voltage range is clearly marked on the casing, even if this means painting on the information. One of the most used of this size of motor is the Meccano electric motor with integral gearbox. There will often be uses for motors of a size likely to be found in domestic equipment and these should be taken into stock whenever they are available. Requirements for power application in a straight line (as opposed to rotation) can be met by electric solenoids. Again, these need to be clearly marked as to electrical input and mechanical output characteristics.

The electric motors themselves need energy and usually this will be at fairly low voltages. Dry batteries can be used but many schools have found power packs (such as Lab-pack or Irwin) to give greater flexibility. Besides supplying electric motors they will also be needed for the electronic modules used in control. One of 8A capacity with ability to supply up to 24V varied in steps and provided with a thermal cut-out will be adequate for most purposes.

At times there will be a need for a source which is self-contained and not dependent on leads. Electric motors with batteries might suffice for light power applications but for others a small internal combustion engine of the size used in lawnmowers may be more suitable. For very light power requirements, rubber strip can store energy either by twisting or stretching in a straight line. Other applications may be better suited by energy storage in springs, usually of the helical variety.

There are many occasions when a fluid flow or pressure is required. For water, several pumps are likely to be needed and those from scrapped domestic spin driers are adequate for many applications. Another type are the circulating pumps from central heating systems. Both these types require secure fixing but where this is not possible or convenient, the self-contained electric submersible pump of the size used for garden fountains is adequate. For air flow, the rear end of a second-hand domestic vacuum cleaner gives a good 'blow' whilst the normal end will provide 'vacuum' sufficient for many purposes. For air pressure, as required for pneumatic control systems, a small air compressor and receiver are essential.

For heat sources, a second hand domestic electric cooker will provide both diffused heating in the oven and more localized heating on the hot plates. Hand-held hair driers provide a more easily directed source of heat but where complete mobility is needed, a gas blowlamp is desirable.

Light sources can be provided by both small and large electric lamps, necessitating a stock of lampholders for these sizes. Associated with these sources are means of directing or focusing. Mirrors and lenses should be on hand, together with means of holding them in a practical manner. Reference has already been made to the use of plastic drain pipes for this under the discussion of structures. Because of the need for robustness, the plated plastic mirrors marketed by Osmiroid are worth considering since they can be obtained in square sheets which can be cut to size and used flat or bent as required.

Transmissions

For many devices, the simple mechanical methods of gears, pulleys and belts can be provided from Meccano parts. For light loads, the plastic gears stocked by model shops are adequate and offer scope for the design and assembly of small gear boxes. For transmission of heavier loads there will be needs for the pulleys and belts available as spares for many domestic appliances. For producing non-standard lengths of belt, it is possible to buy reels of circular section plastic to cut to the desired length and join by heating the ends and pressing together.

One of the deficiencies of the Meccano system is the lack of proper bearing surfaces for the shafts. Hybridex does not have this limitation. For larger transmissions it is essential to have a series of simple plummer blocks to accommodate shafts of a size likely to be encountered in schools technology.

In addition to these mechanical transmission devices, there is likely to be a need for transmission of fluid power necessitating a stock of flexible hose together with appropriate connectors.

Control

This function can be performed at different levels of sophistication from the basic on-off switch or stop-valve to systems involving bi-stable devices and signal amplification. It is worthwhile having a wide variety of control methods available covering mechanical, electrical, electronic and fluid techniques.

Mechanical control will be by elements of transmission systems which have already been discussed, or by systems of guides or linkages, specially made for each application.

Electrical methods will involve simple switches of the one or two-pole variety, rotary switches, variable resistors, relays and microswitches. Time switches of the Venner type with provision for up to 4 pairs of 'on' and 'off' positions in 24 hours also find applications in a number of technological projects. The power packs already described under energy sources provide step control. Continuous control is provided by robust and comparatively cheap controllers sold for model railways. An interesting example of this is the range made by Routier Electronic Engineers and marketed under the name of Brakeman in which the control is moved linearly.

More sophisticated methods may require reed switches, light sensitive devices, triggering circuits and amplifiers. Although electronic devices could be made using discrete components and it is anticipated that there will always be a number of pupils sufficiently able, and interested in developing solutions to specific problems in this way, the majority will merely need to be able to apply the different devices, hence sufficient| complete items should be on hand to enable them to do this. Again it must be emphasized that here we are considering equipment for producing useful solutions that satisfy real needs. This is unlikely to involve using electronic components to reproduce a tested electronic circuit and will not be concerned with examining the principles of electronics. These activities might be included amongst the list of prerequisites for schools technology discussed in the introduction.

Measurement

Evaluation of the effectiveness of the solution to a given problem will involve measurement of some sort but this will be an integral part of many solutions. For example, although from the definition given, studying material properties would be part of the preparation for undertaking schools technology, one of the needs which might be satisfied by this could be for a device to compare properties of different materials. This would entail providing means of measuring, say, the load applied to the material|and the extension produced in it.

For measuring linear dimensions and movements, metre rules, micrometers and dial test indicators (with appropriate stands and clamps) are necessary. For measuring angles and angular movement 360° transparent plastic protractors are useful but many applications require a datum such as that provided by a spirit level. Alternatively a plumb line can be used but as a complete list will utilize simple items likely to be found elsewhere in the school, there is no need to include them here.

Quantities of matter can be compared using kitchen-type scales. Occasions demanding the accuracy of a physical balance seem so few that there is little justification in duplicating the provision of those already existing in the science laboratories. For measurement of forces, a range of spring balances is desirable preferably graduated in newtons to avoid confusion with the oft-encountered graduations in grammes. In many cases it is convenient to obtain a force derived from that of gravity on a vertically hanging mass or load. Sometimes the mass consists of a number of standard, calibrated and marked masses as already discussed under energy sources. On other occasions finer measurements of force application are required and these can be obtained by running water or sand into an appropriately graduated suspended container until the desired phenomenon is observed at which time the container and its contents are transferred to a spring balance to measure the gravitational force on them.

The above are the basic items necessary but often their individual range is considerably extended by the use of magnifying devices such as levers and their incorporation in more elaborate measuring systems.

To measure time, stop clocks are required and events can be counted by mechanical counters actuated by a lever, such as those used for counting revolutions of a bicycle wheel. Measuring rotational speed is conveniently performed by a simple stroboscope and the number of uses for this in schools technology is sufficient to justify one extra to any in the science laboratories.

Temperature measurement usually requires something more robust than glass thermometers. For the normal range of temperatures the thermometers marketed by Osmiroid may be sufficient but these need to be complemented by simple pyrometers for higher ranges.

For electrical measurements, the instruments must be robust even if this means sacrificing some of the accuracy needed in science laboratories. For quick checking of circuits, an instrument of the Avometer type is invaluable.

Check-list

As a check on the items considered above a list is provided in the Appendix. This also provides a section on small tools which is included because often technological activities are undertaken in a room separate from the traditional craft workshop. It is assumed that the production of any special components required will take place in those workshops but that assembly and adjustment will be in the technology area.

The list concentrates on reusable items but it should be noted that in addition to consumable materials such as wood, metal and plastics there will be others needed for technology which would not normally be stocked in the material manipulation areas.

Implications of the check-list

The list suggests items of hardware to help achieve all the learning outcomes specified in the introduction. Only by having this range of equipment will we avoid the tendency for schools technology to be regarded as synonomous with, say, electronics because of the enthusiasm of a particular teacher. Such over-specialization has the disadvantages that:

(a) pupils do not get a sufficiently broad approach to achieve the learning outcomes listed earlier

(b) when that particular teacher leaves, the school may be left with a mass of equipment which does not meet the needs of the next teacher appointed for technology.

Because of the variety of items listed, it is imperative that adequate storage is provided for these in the technology area. The main criterion for the storage should be that any item can be easily located. This means that storage will require more space than can be found under benches or working surfaces and that the building must provide some floor to ceiling wall space (i.e. without windows) against which storage racks or cupboards can be placed.

Many of the items in the list can be obtained as scrap or through agencies such as the Surplus Buying Agency. The kits of Meccano components, items for pneumatic control and electronic modules available from the National Centre for Schools Technology for the Control Technology courses, provide a good basic stock for many of the items in the list.

Although the list is long, it is not intended to provide for the rarely used or unexpected item. When these are needed there must be some financial arrangement whereby the technology teacher can obtain them quickly.

Figure 1

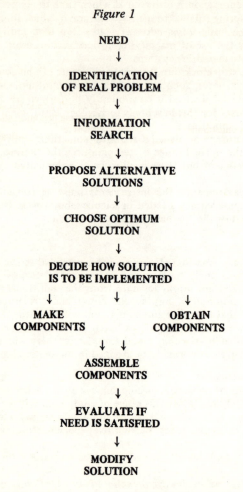

NEED
↓
**IDENTIFICATION
OF REAL PROBLEM**
↓
**INFORMATION
SEARCH**
↓
**PROPOSE ALTERNATIVE
SOLUTIONS**
↓
**CHOOSE OPTIMUM
SOLUTION**
↓
**DECIDE HOW SOLUTION
IS TO BE IMPLEMENTED**
↓   ↓   ↓
**MAKE   OBTAIN
COMPONENTS   COMPONENTS**
↓ ↓
**ASSEMBLE
COMPONENTS**
↓
**EVALUATE IF
NEED IS SATISFIED**
↓
**MODIFY
SOLUTION**

APPENDIX   Check list of basic equipment for schools technology

To provide structures
Meccano parts
Dexion or Handi-angle
Hybridex
Tubes and tubular-fittings
Plastic drain pipes and fittings
Laboratory clamp stands and accessories
G-cramps
Containers (Buckets, oil drums and smaller)
Wheels, castors

To provide energy sources
Power Packs
Electric motors, range of sizes from miniature
    up to ¼ HP
Solenoids
Small internal combustion engine (e.g. lawnmower
    size) with fuel tank
Small water pumps e.g. electric submersible for
    garden fountains
Air compressor and receiver

94

Second-hand vacuum cleaner
Calibrated masses ('Weights')
Strip rubber (for twisted rubber 'motors')
Hair drier
Portable oven and hotplate (or second hand
    domestic cooker)
Gas blow lamp
Lamp holders and lamps
Mirrors, lenses and practical holding system

To provide transmissions
Gears, Pulleys, Belts, e.g. Meccano, plastic gears
    as sold for models, + larger sizes e.g. those
    available as spares for domestic electrical
    washers etc.
Plummer blocks
Flexible hose and hose connections

To provide control
One and two-pole electrical switches
Rotary switches
Microswitches
Variable resistors
Electric controllers (as used for model railways)
Time switches
Reed switches
Amplifiers
Trigger circuits
Light sensitive devices
Pneumatic single & double acting cylinders
Pneumatic 3 - and 5-port valves
Pneumatic flow switches & bi-stable devices
Pneumatic reservoirs

For measuring
Metre rules

Micrometer
Dial test indicators and stands
360° transparent plastic protractors
Spirit level
Kitchen-type scales
Spring balances of various sizes, graduated in
    newtons
Pressure gauges
Stopclocks
Mechanical counter
Scalar
Stroboscope
Thermometers
Pyrometer
Graduated plastic buckets
Measuring jugs and cylinders
Voltmeter
Ammeter   with appropriate shunts
Avometer
Oscilloscopes

Small tools (mainly for assembly)
Hand power drills 110v.
Drills
Soldering irons
Wire strippers
Pliers
Small screwdrivers
Heat sinks
Scissors
Medium screwdrivers
Files
Hacksaw
Spanners up to size for pipe systems
Tenon saw

References
1   Marshall, A. *School Technology in Action,* EUP/The Open University Press.